Youth and Values: Getting Self Together

Carl A. Elder

BROADMAN PRESS
Nashville, Tennessee

© Copyright 1978 · Broadman Press.

4253–26

ISBN: 0–8054–5326–1

Dewey Decimal Classification: 248.83

Subject headings: CHRISTIAN LIFE // YOUTH

Library of Congress Catalog Card Number: 76–58063

Printed in the United States of America

This book is affectionately dedicated to

my first grandchild

Heather Marie Hall

*who was born during the writing
of this book and who, in the providence
of God, will grow to become
a teenager*

Acknowledgments

The author is particularly grateful to his dear wife, Wynona Elder, Ed.D., who served as coauthor of this book by contributing several chapters and by reading and editing the entire manuscript. Grateful appreciation is given to Mrs. Sue Elder for typing and proofreading the manuscript and for other helpful suggestions.

Grateful acknowledgment is extended to friends and associates for their encouragement during the long months of writing.

Finally, the author would like to express his feelings of gratitude to his children, Mark, Carla, Mona, and Mona's husband, Norm Hall, who exhibited so much understanding and concern during the writing of this book.

The material on page 37 is adapted from Louis Raths, Merrill Harmin, and Sidney Simon, *Values and Teaching* (Columbus: Charles E. Merrill, 1966), pp. 38–39.

Contents

Introduction

You are in the midst of growing and becoming an adult. You are a physical, emotional, spiritual, and rational being. There is something special and unique about you. You have values, feelings, and attitudes. There is not another person just like you anywhere.

You have reached the place in life where you make more and more of your decisions. You make personal value judgments about the way you want to live your life. You may find yourself clarifying your values because of the moral decisions you face. This is a natural thing. You may be pressured by your peers to decide something that is against your values and Christian commitments.

You are pulled one way by your friends and another way by your family and church. You wonder what changes you need to make in your life. You think about your life goals. You sometimes doubt your faith in God. At times you may feel that nothing is right for you.

This book is designed to get you to think about you and your values. Section I, the first four chapters, deals with this aspect of you as a person—someone uniquely important. Section II, chapters 5 through 8, deals with your values and Christian commitment. Such questions as, What can I know about God? What do I know about the church? How does the Bible affect me? and What does Christian love mean to me? will be discussed.

Section III, chapters 9 through 14, discusses the concept of living with your values. How do I get along with others? How do I value myself? Where do I go from here? These and other major questions are emphasized.

The book is written with the hope that it will help you to become aware of your values and act on them. It is designed to help you face personal decisions by raising many questions that you face all of the time. If this book helps you know what you value, helps you know yourself, helps your relationships with others, or helps you get life together, then it was more than worth the effort.

PART I

VALUES AND ME

1

What Do I Know About Me?

"My parents do not understand me and my needs." (Boy, 16.)

"It's hard for me to make friends." (Girl, 15.)

"I'm just not as smart as other kids." (Boy, 13.)

"I think I am growing too fast." (Boy, 14.)

"I am embarrassed because I am more developed than my friends." (Girl, 13.)

"I sometimes find it very hard to talk with God, yet I go to church all the time." (Girl, 17.)

Do these statements sound like thoughts you have had about yourself? You have probably wondered about the growth taking place in your body. You may have questioned why you had such strong feelings about a person or a thing. At other times you have wondered about other people, your friends, your family. You have thought about whether they have doubts about themselves. You have also looked for answers to questions about God, the church, the Bible.

You are a very special person. You are different from

everyone else in the world. Out of all the thousands of possibilities that existed at the time of your conception, you became you. After you were born you began experiencing the world in your own unique way. This also contributed to making you the person that you are. You are you—no one else can possibly be just like you.

Although unique in your physical makeup, thoughts, and feelings, you share with every other person a period of time called adolescence (teenage years). During this time you experience the physical growth that takes you from childhood to adulthood. You also experience a deepening of feelings. You learn many new and exciting things about the world and about God. You experience new relationships with other boys and girls and with adults. All these things as part of your experience are also part of the experience of millions of other teenagers. But no one will ever experience them in exactly the same way that you do.

For this reason, you may be searching for help with understanding just who you are as a person. You may be looking for answers to questions about your needs (those urges within you that cause you to act in certain ways). You may feel that some very strange things are happening to you which you cannot understand. It may help to know that others are also experiencing these strange happenings and are trying to understand them.

To make things a little simpler, think of yourself as being made up of five parts neatly fitted into a whole. These five parts will be named the Physical You, the Emotional You, the Social You, the Intellectual You, and the Spiritual You. Remember that these do not operate alone. They operate together, but each one has its own functions and needs. Every part of you must grow and develop. Neglect any part and you are kept from becoming the "whole person" or "the real you" you want to become.

Acceptance of each part of you is a big and important step. Acceptance requires understanding. To gain some understanding, look at each part of you.

The Physical You

Physical changes are taking place in your body. The development of breasts, a larger penis, hair under the arms and in the genital area of the body, and, for boys, on the face—these are some of the noticeable differences between you *now* and you five years ago. Yet there may be some teenagers reading this who have noticed none of these things. It is important to understand that physically your body is changing from a child's body to an adult's body. For some individuals the change is slow and gradual. For others it is abrupt and rapid. But it happens to everyone—sooner or later. The changes will result in your own unique body.

The color of your eyes and hair were determined when you were conceived. To a large extent the size of your body was also determined at conception. These things were determined by the unique combination of characteristics you received from your mother and father. They could not choose these things ahead of time, just as they could not choose whether they would have a boy or a girl. Through God's creation you are what you are, and you are great and very special to him.

A very important part of the Physical You is your sexuality. As a result of the creative process, God gave you maleness or femaleness. As a male, you have certain sexual characteristics. As a female, you have certain sexual characteristics. These develop through the teenage years and prepare you for very special sexual functions.

Who you are sexually concerns most young men and young women. A good understanding of sexuality is essential to health and happiness. Consider the following statements:

1. Your body is the result of the miracle of birth.

2. God created male and female—and said that his creation was good. Therefore, sexuality is beautiful, clean, and good.

3. The purpose of sexuality is that a male and a female may enjoy each other in a relationship of love and marriage. Another purpose of sexuality for some is that they can bring children into the world to love.

4. Your sexuality is expressed as a need to be close to someone of the opposite sex. At times this need seems urgent. How you use it is your choice. To use it responsibly and well requires courage, self-control, and understanding.

The Emotional You

While you have noticed physical changes taking place in your body, you may have been aware that your feelings (emotions) are changing, too. Your feelings about your body are changing. When you look around and see the differences between you and your friends, you feel uneasy. You wonder whether you are normal.

You may feel confused about your parents. Now you are almost an adult, and they still treat you like a child. You feel disappointed when they fail to recognize your need for independence. You want desperately to make your own decisions and feel trapped when you are not allowed to do so.

There are times when you want everyone to leave you alone. All you want to do is stay in your room and listen to your latest records. At other times you want to be with your friends.

You may become aware of a feeling like fear. It is not that you are afraid of anything in particular, but you feel an uneasiness. This may be felt as "butterflies in the stomach," dryness of the mouth, sweaty palms, dizziness, or weakness. These feelings are sometimes there because you are afraid of the unknown. You feel that something bad is about to happen, yet you do not know what it is or what to do about it. Sometimes you become aware of these feelings just before you have to get up in front of a class to speak. If you are an athlete, you may feel this way before a big game. Anxiety is a normal feeling. Everyone experiences this emotion at times. Recognizing it and realizing that it will not last forever are important in getting rid of this distressing feeling.

The Emotional You expresses itself in your behavior. When you are angry, you will act in angry ways. You may yell at your parents, slam a door, or drive the car too fast. When you feel disappointed or sad you may cry. Some ways that we express our emotions are suitable; other ways are not.

The Emotional You is aware of becoming involved with other people. Strong feelings of liking another person or even feelings of love are common to teenagers. These feelings also get involved with your sexuality. Sexual feelings, urges to be close to and touch a person of the opposite sex, are especially strong. The feelings are natural and normal. How to express them is sometimes confusing and difficult.

All these feelings—disappointment, confusion, uneasiness, dependence, independence, love, joy, hate, anger, and many others—are a normal part of the Emotional You. You are becoming more aware of these feelings and what they mean. You are also learning that while sometimes you can express your feelings, at other times you cannot. The important thing is that you accept your feelings as OK. Then you will be able to learn to express them in normal and suitable ways.

The Social You

Most people are born into a family who provides for their needs as infants and children. The family provides the food, shelter, and clothing a child needs as he grows. The family also provides love and security. As you have grown you have depended upon significant people in your life for love and protection. These significant people were probably mother, father, grandparents, brothers and sisters, teachers at school or at church, and friends.

When you approach the teenage years, your friends become increasingly important. Your peers (individuals near your same age) provide standards for your behavior. It suddenly seems very important to wear overalls if that is what your peers are wearing. It may be that not everyone is wearing overalls; but if someone whom you particularly admire wears them, it seems extremely important to you that you wear overalls too.

The influence of your peers is felt not just in the way you dress or comb your hair; it is also felt in the kind of music you listen to and the kind of posters you put on the walls of your room.

Socially, the teenage years are a time for reaching out. You will come into contact with more and more people. You will seek relationships with persons of the same sex and with persons of the opposite sex. You will seek relationships with more adults. As you relate to these people, you will learn more about yourself and the kind of person you are. What these people think of you will be important, but your most important task is to decide what you think of yourself.

The Intellectual You

If someone were to ask you what your biggest problem is, your answer might have something to do with school.

Grades, learning, deciding which subjects to take, and teachers are all part of the frustrations of getting an education. In the United States great value is placed on education. It is generally thought that the more education one has, the better off that person will be.

The Intellectual You is made up of thoughts, ideas, and opinions. As you grow and go through life, your ideas and thoughts grow and change. Your ability to think for yourself, to solve problems, and to make decisions grows. During the teenage years this ability grows rapidly.

All teenagers differ in their capacities for thinking and learning. For some the ability to read, study, and learn in school comes very easily. These students generally enjoy school and will probably continue on to college or in other kinds of schooling following high school graduation.

For some teenagers, school is very difficult and becomes a real drag. Reading and gaining knowledge from books or from listening to teachers is very hard. Some of these students may enjoy the classes in school where they can do things with their hands. They prefer subjects such as cooking, art, woodworking, auto mechanics, and printing. Some students prefer these subjects although language arts, history, and science are not difficult for them.

Every person is unique in his way of learning. Some learn best through reading. Some learn best by hearing explanations or engaging in discussions. Some learn best by doing something with their hands. Others learn best by combinations of all these things. How do you learn best? Your answer to that question may help you determine the subjects you take in school. It may also help you determine what you will do when you get out of high school. You may need a counselor to help you answer that question and to apply the answer to your other decisions about what you want from life.

Learning and thinking takes place in other places besides school. Your experiences in the world around you help you make many discoveries and learn many things.

A definite part of the Intellectual You is your desire to help make decisions that affect you directly. As part of a family, a school class, or any other group, you very much feel the need for being able to decide when you will come home after a date, or what the penalty will be for cheating or other misbehavior at school.

Intellectually, you may be ready for these kinds of decisions; yet the adults around you may continue to make these rules for you. *Why?* you may ask yourself. There may be several reasons. The main reason seems to be tied up with the responsibility that goes with decision making. When you demonstrate your ability to take responsibility and to live with the consequences of your decisions, adults are more ready to pass on to you the role of decision making. Later chapters will deal with this important issue.

The Spiritual You

For many, the most difficult aspect of ourselves to understand is our spiritual self. As creations of God, he has given us a longing or a desire to have a relationship with him. We do this by knowing and accepting Jesus Christ as God's Son and our Savior.

Worshiping God is a part of our desire for a relationship with him. When you attend worship services, participate in the singing, giving an offering, listening to the sermon, and responding to the message you have heard, you have partly filled this desire. You know, though, that there are places other than the sanctuary of the church where you feel close to God and worship him. Many teenagers participate in and enjoy retreats. These usually take place in some setting where the young people can be close to nature and can feel and commune with God there. Anywhere you are you can talk with and worship God. The Spiritual You will lead you to do this as you listen and pay attention to the urges inside you.

Fellowship with other people is an important part of our relationship with God. He expects us to not only respond to him but to respond to others. As we love God we will also love other people and want to help them. When you attend church services, you have opportunities to reach out to others who are trying to learn about God and have a relationship with him. That helps you to know you are not alone. There are other believers who would like to get to know God better.

In other chapters of this book you will get a better understanding of the Spiritual You and your relationship to God, Christ, the church, and the Bible.

The Whole You

In this chapter you have read about the various aspects of you as a person. To understand yourself better is to be able to understand how you develop as a person physically, emotionally, intellectually, socially, and spiritually. Everything you do as a person affects every part of you because you are a whole person; and every part acts together in every thing you do.

An example of this is church attendance. Physically, your body is there—you get up, get dressed, eat breakfast, either walk or ride to church, sit in a pew, sing, stand, and do many other motions that are purely physical. While you do these things you are thinking. You may be thinking about the fun you had last night, or you may be thinking about the pastor's sermon and how it applies to you. You are also feeling some things. You may be feeling happy that you can once again see your friends. You may be feeling resentment that you had to get up early on Sunday morning after only a few hours of sleep. You are socially involved with other teenagers and adults during this time. Spiritually, you are worshiping God.

You may not be aware of all these things at one time, but all or some of these things are taking place in you during every activity. Learning to be aware of the whole person that you are is what this book is all about.

OPEN-ENDED STATEMENTS

"About Me"

Complete the following statements about yourself.

1. I like myself because _____
   _____.

2. I make friends easily because _____
   _____.

3. I think I am attractive because _____
   _____.

4. I take care of my body because _____
   _____.

5. I think I am a good student because _____
   _____.

6. I get along with others because _____
   _____.

7. I am happy because _____
   _____.

2

What Do I Know About My Values?

"No one ever asked me about my values." (Girl,13.)

"What do I value? Man, I don't know what you are talking about." (Boy, 15.)

"Youth is the period of building up in habits, and hopes, and faiths." (Ruskin.)

"My values should guide my behavior." (Girl, 16.)

"I get my values from my parents." (Boy, 12.)

Tom and Betty are older high school students and have been dating for about six weeks. Tom decides to take some beer along on their next date and drink it after the movie. Here's the conversation that took place between them.

"Betty, I have some cold beer. Let's drink some."

"Tom, I have never tasted beer. And from what I hear it's not that good."

"It's not that bad; come on, have some and try it."

"I don't know, Tom. My family just never messes around with beer and that stuff."

"Don't be stuck-up. You can do what you please."

"Yes, Tom, you are right. I can do what I please, and

I choose not to drink the beer."

"What's wrong with drinking a can of beer now and then?"

"There may be nothing wrong for you to drink now and then, but I don't think that I want to—not just yet, anyway."

"OK, let's go get a coke or something."

"Thanks, Tom, for not insisting that I drink that beer."

"Let's just drop the whole thing. I'm sorry I brought the stuff."

This short real-life story points up your need to take a look at your values. What are values? Who needs values? What are your values? Why do values differ among people? Where do you get your values? These and other questions will be considered in this chapter.

What Are Values?

A value is something that has worth and is desirable. A value represents something important to human existence. To value is to rate something such as a person, an idea, a thing, a belief, or a principle very highly. For instance, you may value courtesy, while your friend believes that it is unimportant. That is, it has no value for him as a standard of conduct to guide his life. Or your mother may value promptness, but you may think getting to the breakfast table every morning at a certain time makes no difference.

Values are those elements or principles that help you decide how to use your life. Your values assist you in determining levels of goodness, worth, and beauty. For example, if someone told you he disliked a certain person because he or she was dishonest, then that person would possess the value of honesty. Although people do not possess all of the same values, the values you hold are important because they influence the way you live. Values can be viewed as building blocks for the construction of a meaningful life.

Who Needs Values?

Even though you now have some knowledge of what values are, you still may want to ask, "Who needs values?" That is a question that you will have to answer for yourself. To answer it to your satisfaction, you might take another look at yourself.

You are becoming more aware of your basic desires and needs. You are in the midst of body changes that occur in early teens. You are experiencing different levels of physical maturity.

You are concerned with how you look and what you wear. Your feelings are deep-seated and many times strangely silent. You have secrets and private daydreams. Life to you is full of mysteries and frustrations.

You ache on the inside as a result of those new and sometimes frightening desires. Your emotions can erupt instantly. At one moment you can be laughing and at the next be in tears. You hurt in places you cannot name and feel sick when nothing physical can be found wrong.

You are more knowledgeable than any generation known to man. You have talents, skills, and energy that defy the imagination. Yet, in all your affluence, you are faced with anxiety, frustration, guilt, and boredom. You and your friends have increased in numbers, but perhaps you have not felt a corresponding increase in self-identity, security, and independence.

You desire security, but not a security based only on money and material things. You feel the need of a secure homelife where you are accepted and wanted. You want to be loved, but not necessarily hugged all the time. Just knowing that someone is there, someone who cares, has real meaning for you.

You want to know more about yourself. You are beginning to feel your sex drive, and this is both stimulating and frustrating. You feel the need of sincere guidance and understanding to see you through this period of life. You want to know more about your own sexuality.

You have a desire not only to be accepted, to have a sense of security, to know more about yourself; but you want your life to have meaning and purpose.

Back to the question "Who needs values?" If you want to be in control of your desires and drives, then *you* need values. If you want a better understanding and acceptance of yourself, then *you* need values. If you desire some basic moral principles to guide your life, then *you* need values. If you want your life to have meaning and purpose in relationship to the world around you, then *you* need values.

You might disagree with the basic moral values of society such as honesty, loyalty, respect, affection, faith, and responsibility. You might adopt your own values. That is your decision. You may accept some of these and reject others. That's still your decision. No one is going to police you all of your life. You must live your own life and answer for your own behavior. But you will have values. No person can live in a vacuum.

Why Do Values Differ in Our Society?

Accepting the fact that we all need and have values, we ask, "Why do values differ in our society?" One reason for differing values is that our society is made up of many different cultural influences. This nation was established by people from many countries of the world.

Our society is made up of many ethnic groups. Each ethnic group's heritage and customs may be different from other groups. Many ethnic groups are attempting to preserve their culture. In most major cities there are newspapers printed in Spanish, Japanese, Italian, and other non-English languages. There are private schools that teach the children the customs and language of their particular ethnic group.

Various ethnic groups observe different holidays with religious significance. Each of these ethnic groups takes very seriously many of the customs and values of their ancestors. In America, these ethnic groups have definitely influenced our culture. For instance, in every major city there are Chinese and Italian restaurants. The Christmas tree is an old German tradition. Have you noticed the influence of the African beat on some music you hear and like to move to? In a nation such as America, are the values and customs of one group the only right ones?

Although some values and customs differ between ethnic groups, there are still certain values that cut across racial and cultural barriers. These values include love, honesty, loyalty, courage, respect, recognition, wealth, power, well-being, enlightenment, skill, and faith.

What Are My Values?

Have you ever written down on a piece of paper what you value? Or has someone asked you what you value? Most teenagers like you value their friends, their families, and special personal possessions. Just about every teenager can name several people or things that mean a great deal to him, but what about those values that guide your everyday behavior? To see what you value, stop right now and take the following Values Preference Inventory.

Look at the list of values. Take your time and rank them 1—8 by placing a 1 in the blank before the value you prize most, a 2 by the next value you prize most, and a 3 by the next, until you have ranked all the values according to your preference. Remember, this is not a test. All of the values listed are held by most people in our society, but they place a different importance on them from time to time. Directly under each of the values are other words to help describe their meaning.

Rank 1–8   Human Values

_____   *Wealth*
Money, Property, Food

_____   *Love*
Affection, Kindness, Tenderness

_____   *Rectitude*
Honesty, Trust, Fair Play

_____   *Well Being*
Health, Happiness, Contentment

_____   *Skill*
Ability, Talent, Ingenuity

_____   *Respect*
Recognition, Honor, Courtesy

_____   *Enlightenment*
Knowledge, Understanding, Education

_____   *Power*
Influence, Decision Making, Leadership

After you finish, take a piece of paper and write down the values in order, beginning with the value you ranked 1. Now look at the list and see if the way you live and act corresponds to the way you ranked the values. If it does, then you have found out what values are really important to you. If it does not, then you have found that you have some value conflicts—that is, *saying* you prize a value very highly but not demonstrating that belief in your behavior.

Knowing what you value and why is very important

as you face the task of everyday living. Your values act as guides to help you make the right choices when there is no one around to tell you what you must do. Values are much like beacon lights guiding you safely through the rough places of life. Values are always there because they belong to you.

Beliefs and Commitments

Your beliefs and commitments are major influences on your values. Your belief in God, taken very seriously, will influence you in acknowledging certain values. For example, the value of worship will mean more and more to you as you grow older. The value of living a clean moral life under the lordship of Jesus Christ will give you self-esteem. The value of accepting all people as being created by God will help you become a more understanding person. Your beliefs in God, Christ, the church, the created order, and your fellowman will create in you a real purpose for living. Your beliefs help you put into everyday living the values you hold and cherish. It is very important that you continue to develop and broaden the things you believe in.

Personal commitments play a large role in helping you form personal values. When you are committed to keeping your body pure for the one you someday may marry, that commitment helps you say no to the pressures of sex. You are committed to getting a good education, and that motivates you to study. Being committed to something is usually thought of as being willing to sacrifice your time and energy for that something.

Consider the following statements in the light of your own values, beliefs, and commitments:

1. Select your own life's purpose.
2. Set personal goals that have meaning to you and

will give a sense of self-worth. Your potentials can guide you.

3.   Select your life's vocation—taking into consideration your personal skills and desires.

4.   Limit your concern for immediate satisfaction in the areas of sex, property, and money. Time and your own personal growth will help you eventually satisfy these basic desires and drives.

These suggestions are based on your personal values, commitments, and beliefs. They merit your sincere consideration. The choice at times will be difficult. You will make mistakes. But through all your living and searching, your values, commitments, and beliefs will play a large role in your development as a whole person. Through this process of personal growth you will find out more about yourself and what your values are.

Where Do I Get My Values?

Have you ever wondered just where you get your values? Of course you know that you were not born with values. As a baby you were incapable of moral or rational decisions. But as you grew you were taught values, and those around you modeled their values. In this way you began to acquire a set of values, which would be the guiding principles for directing your life. Basically values come from three distinct sources: religion, family, and society.

Religion

Your religious beliefs tend to dictate to you some basic values of moral and spiritual importance. Your religion seeks to point you to the truth about your life, death, and destiny. Your religious convictions and beliefs attempt to help you understand the meaning of life and the standards through which the good life is found. The part that religion plays in influencing your values depends on your personal commitment to your religious beliefs.

Religion does not make a difference in the lives of some teenagers because they do not hold to any religious convictions and beliefs. To other teenagers religion is a vital part of their life experiences. A large majority of the young people today admit that their religious beliefs and convictions help them to accept some basic moral values.

Some examples of your values that come from your religious beliefs are brotherly love, service to others, and respect for the rights and property of others. Even if you do not have religious beliefs or religious upbringing, you probably have been influenced by religion anyway. You can see this influence when you compare the Ten Commandments and other religious principles with many of our laws.

Family

Another way you acquire your values is from your family. As a young child most of your values came from your family. Those who have studied the influence of the family on children agree that the family molds attitudes— feelings toward a particular fact or condition—of the child. They further agree that by molding attitudes and by shaping understanding of oneself, the family passes on its moral values of right and wrong from generation to generation.

This process of passing on moral values to children is accomplished by positive relationships between parent and child. Can you remember, when you were younger, how good you felt to have parents care for you and show deep concern for your welfare in all kinds of situations? Can you remember all the love and care they gave you?

Your parents helped you acquire values by teaching and by living before you as models.

As you are growing older you are finding that at times your values and those of your parents are different—that is, they are in conflict with one another. This is part of growing up. These conflicts can be worked out through a clear understanding of the situation and respect for each other. As a young person you cannot expect your parents to give up basic moral and spiritual values they have held all their lives. You would not want them to do this because they would appear to be hypocritical— pretending to be what they are not. But on the other hand, parents need to understand that many times they can see your point of view without sacrificing any of their values or principles. Remember, for good or bad, your families influence your life by giving you many of your values and shaping many of your attitudes.

Society

Your experience with people in society shapes your moral values. Society means all people, but your relationships for the most part are with your peers. You may find out that some of the values you and your family hold differ from those of your peers. What do you do then? Do you discard your values and accept those of your peers? Or do you examine your own values in the light of the new so you will be able to make meaningful decisions?

As you face society in general and your peers in particular, the values given to you by your religious faith and by your family will be fully tested. Your values grow out of your experiences. And it is by these experiences you learn what is right and best for you. Also, as you grow you will reexamine your values in the light of your changing experiences. The process of examining your values will make them more meaningful to you if you decide to keep them.

You and Your Values

It is not too difficult to understand values. You need values to guide your life and your behavior in society. Because this society is made up of many ethnic groups, there are many different values among people. Through the experience of living and growing, you come to know what you value. By the time you become a teenager, you begin to realize where you get your values—from religion, family, and society. Along the way you will be encouraged by your own values about how to live and act. You are a very important person. You have worth and dignity. You have talents, skills, desires, emotions, and needs. When you hold onto a set of values, your life can have purpose and meaning. Your values will help you channel the whole you in ways that are both happy and productive.

WHAT WOULD I DO?

"The Twenty-Dollar Bill"

Your mother asked you to go to the store for her. You left the supermarket, and as you started to the car you counted your change. You discovered that the cashier gave you twenty dollars too much.

What will you do?

Why?

What values are important to you in making your decision?

What might be the results of your decision?

What other choices do you have?

3

How Do I Make Decisions?

"It's hard to be a teenager because everybody seems to know what I need and want more than I do." (Teenage boy.)

"Sometimes it is hard for me to decide what I must do." (Teenage girl.)

"Youth is the opportunity to do something and become somebody." (T. T. Munger.)

"Youth is the time you want to live like an adult, but on an allowance of $3.00 per week." (Author unknown.)

"It seems everybody is trying to tell me what I must do." (Teenage boy.)

Making decisions in today's society can be very complex. It's hard and very frustrating for you to know which way to decide. And you really are not sure just how things will turn out. You do not possess the power to give you a peek at the future. Sometimes you might wonder if you will ever make it past your nineteenth birthday. Making decisions is part of life and growing. This chapter will seek to help you gain a better insight into what judging is, what a value judgment is, how decisions are made, what value theories are, and how you make personal value judgments.

Making Decisions

As teenagers you are faced with many different kinds of decisions. The following quotations by teenagers will help you see some of the many decisions you have to make.

"I will choose my own friends."

"It's my money. I will buy what I like."

"But I don't like that dress."

"I am going out for football."

"Sex—not me. That's for married people."

"I am trying to find a part-time job."

"Me? Play in the band! Man, have you flipped?"

"Kiss on the first date? Not me!"

"I go to church—my religion is important to me."

"Smoking is a drag."

"Do you think I should run for student council?"

"I am not going to mess up my life by popping pills."

"I can't cut the booze—it's dumb."

You can see that you are making decisions about friends, money, dress, sports, dating, sex, involvement, religion, smoking, drugs, part-time employment, responsibility, and drinking. As you grow older you are faced with other decisions. You must decide about full-time employment. You must decide about further training in a vocational area of your choice. If you decide to enter college, you must decide which college. Some of you who are older teenagers are even thinking about marriage— that's a big decision.

Just about every time you turn around you are making decisions. You see a commercial on TV and decide to try the product. You hear a song on the radio, and you buy the record. A friend offers you a "joint" (marijuana cigarette), and you must decide what to do. Some decisions are easy to make and some are hard. One thing is clear: You cannot escape making decisions about your life and how you are going to live it.

Judging

Before you make a decision to do something, you will no doubt judge whether it is right for you. What is judging? What do you know about judging as a part of decision making? Judging is an act of estimating, predicting, grading, and adjudicating (giving a fair judgment based on justice). The act of judging implies the use of some standards, grounds, rules, principles, and reasons when absolute knowledge is absent. Looking at this definition one step at a time might help you gain a better understanding of its importance to decision making.

Judging is estimating. You are estimating when you look at a room and judge the distance from side to side. You are estimating when you say that Tom can run the mile in about five minutes. You are estimating when you state that your bed will fit into a certain space without having first measured to see if it would. Being good at estimating depends on the experience and knowledge you have.

Judging is predicting. "Joe won't show up for the car-wash project," you state to the group. Why are you so sure Joe won't show up? It may be because Joe has said that he would on other projects and he never has helped yet. You make your predictions of Joe's not coming on your past experience and knowledge of him. You are not absolutely certain he will not show up to help, but you are pretty sure. Predicting is part of judging and helps you to arrive at certain decisions.

Judging is grading. Can you see where judging is grading in the examples below?

"John is a good judge of dogs."

"Debbie is a good judge of horses."

"Frank is a good judge of cattle."

"Faye is a good judge of apple pie."

Grading and ranking take place when something is judged to be better than the next. When you are grading something you are applying certain standards, based on experience, to render a good judgment. You use grading a lot when you shop for clothes or other personal items. The decision to buy is usually based on the quality of the item. You are the one who grades the quality.

Judging is adjudicating. Don't let that big word throw you. It simply means giving a fair judgment based on justice. For example, you may be:

—good at refereeing a game of football

—a good judge in settling disputes

—a fair judge in calling a basketball game.

The examples indicate more than grading, predicting, or estimating. They take into account that one must know the rules of the game and have had some experience to be able to render a fair decision. This aspect of judging is very important when you are considering serious decisions.

Judging is not guessing.   You are now aware of what judging is and how being able to judge properly will guide you in making decisions. Remember, guessing is not judging. According to the dictionary, guessing is the act of forming an opinion of something at random without having certain evidence. You are asked how many pennies are in a certain jar. You state that there are five hundred. You made a guess, unless you had counted them previously.

You can see, then, that guessing is based on a hunch or conjecture without the use of reasons, grounds, or principles. Judging is one thing and guessing is another. This raises another question—what is a value judgment?

What Is a Value Judgment?

A value judgment is a decision or opinion based on an object or idea that has meaning and worth to you. Value judgments are not subjective—that is, they are not made on personal feelings and preferences alone. You might consider your reasons, grounds, principles, and knowledge for making value judgments.

Suppose you decide not to try beer or liquor. You make your value judgment based on more than just a preference but on reasons, grounds, principles, and knowledge. You know that it has been reported that beer and liquor can be harmful to the body. But what you don't know for certain is how it will affect you. You value your health. You value your self-esteem. You make a value judgment not to drink because your well-being is important to you.

In a real sense, making value judgments has to do with making moral (good or bad for me) or ethical (right or wrong for me) decisions. There is a process by which you can know how to make personal value decisions.

What Is the Decision-making Process?

There are at least six steps in the process of making a decision. Study each step as listed below.

1. You face a problem.
2. You gather information—both opinion and fact—about your problem.
3. You write down or think about the different solutions and their consequences to your problem.
4. You measure your own values in the light of each possible solution.
5. You come to a decision and feel that it is right for you. You are proud of your choice.

6. You put your decision into action. It becomes a part of your behavior.

To illustrate the decision-making process, suppose you are trying to make a decision that is very important to you. You are now faced with a problem. For example, should I smoke? You look first at your information—fact and opinion. You ask yourself some questions. Why do people smoke? What do the experts say about smoking? Will smoking harm my health? Will my smoking hurt others?

Now you are ready to think about all the alternatives or possible solutions to your problem. Should I smoke at all? Should I smoke just on certain occasions? Should I smoke now or wait until I am older? Should I smoke by myself? After you have looked at all possible solutions, you will then consider the consequences of each one. Will smoking hurt me physically? Will I lose friends if I decide to smoke or if I decide not to smoke? What will my friends think of me? What will my teachers think of me? What will my parents think of me? Will I get into trouble if I smoke openly?

The next step in arriving at a decision is to weigh your personal values. That is, you will look at your values in the light of your problem: Should I smoke? In looking at your values, remember that you are seeking help in achieving your life's highest purpose and meaning. For example, which do you value most: your health? your feelings? your parents? your friends?

You finally reach a decision. You select one of the solutions. Are you happy about the choice? Are you proud that you decided the way you did? What can you do if you find out that you are not happy with your decision? Will you go back and choose another possible solution to your problem that might make you happy? Last, to make a real decision you must put it into action—do something with your choice. Should you smoke? You must decide.

What Is the Valuing Process?

Another process that might help you in making decisions is the valuing process. The valuing process is based on three areas of your life—choosing, prizing, and acting. It is very similar to the decision-making process we just discussed. You might find it easier to remember when you are faced with difficult decisions. A brief summary follows:

Choosing

1. You make your choices freely.
2. Discover all your alternatives—possible solutions—when faced with choices.
3. Consider each alternative—examining the possible consequences of each.

Prizing

4. Consider what you prize and cherish.
5. Be happy about your choice—willing to let others know about it.

Acting

6. Do something with your choice.
7. Let your action become a part of your life.

If you can remember *choosing, prizing,* and *acting* when faced with decisions, you stand a chance of making wise value judgments. This process allows you ample freedom. You are still free to make your own choices and decide for yourself.

What Are Value Theories?

In society there are three major value theories or systems of rules and principles. These systems of rules, viewpoints, or principles guide individuals in making personal judgments based on values.

The value theories are easier to understand if they are in outline form.

Objective Theory

People who accept this point of view believe that:

1.   There exists but one perfect set of values.
2.   These values exist in the world apart from man. Man did not create them or cause them to come into being.
3.   Man through his capacity to think finds these values.
4.   These values are binding on all men at all times and in all places.
5.   These values never change.

If you hold this point of view, you would feel it wrong for all men to cheat and steal. You would agree that it is right for all men to love, be kind, and help others. The strength of this viewpoint takes into account the welfare of others.

Subjective Theory

Those who hold to this point of view would act so as to seek their own pleasure or happiness. They hold that:

1.   Values are always a matter of personal preference.
2.   The individual must decide for himself.
3.   Values are not binding.
4.   Values are man-made.
5.   Values change as your feelings change.

For example, if it would not be pleasurable for you to help your friend mow his lawn, then you are under no obligation to do it. The strength of this viewpoint toward values is that it gives you the freedom to choose your own values. Its basic weakness is selfishness—one is concerned too much for his own self.

Relative Theory

This view is in between the other two. While it rejects a perfect set of values existing apart from man, it is not selfish in its dealings toward man. The main points of this view are:

1. Values are of human invention.
2. Values are objective—but only after they have been tried and proven to be in the best interest of mankind.
3. Values are not absolute.
4. Values are not binding unless man accepts them to be.
5. Values change as man and his society change.
6. Values exist only in relation to other values.

This viewpoint is tolerant of the feelings and attitudes of others. This is one of its major strengths. Its weakness lies in the rejection of a perfect set of values created by God and designed to be the guiding force in man's behavior.

An example of an eternal value is found in Jesus' saying, "Thou shalt *love* the Lord thy God with all thy heart, and with all thy soul, and with all thy mind. This is the first great commandment. And the second is like unto it, Thou shalt *love* thy neighbor as thyself" (Matt. 22:37–39, author's italics).

The value of love is a universal principle for all mankind to follow. Your moral and spiritual development depends on your giving and receiving love—love from God, love for God, and love for man.

You will understand that from time to time you will move back and forth between these three different value theories. Sometimes your decision will be based on God's eternal value of love. At other times you will find yourself deciding for your personal pleasure. And at other times you might find yourself rejecting absolute value for man's values. You will decide which value theory will be basic to your life and will guide your behavior.

How Can I Make Personal Value Judgments?

Some of the value judgments you make are everyday decisions. Decisions as to what to wear, what to do with your free time, when to study, and other value judgments direct daily living. But other value judgments are more serious. You are faced with moral decisions that have far greater importance than simple routine decisions.

Some of these decisions are life-changing decisions. How you decide about some things can alter your lifestyle, change your friends, discourage your parents, and create a whole new set of problems for yourself.

Your value judgments on the following issues could be life-changing for you. Should I drink? Should I smoke? Who will I marry? What about sex before I marry? Should I obey my parents? Are all people created equally? Should I try drugs? Does it matter if I love people? Should I be loyal to my country? Should I obey the laws? Does it matter if I believe in God?

When you make value judgments about such issues as these, you come to grips with the reality of life and living. How, then, do you make personal value judgments? There are several steps you might want to consider. These steps seek to put into focus what this chapter has all been about.

1.   Understand you will make many decisions as you live out your life.

2.   Know the difference between a value judgment and a preference.

3.   Master the process of decision-making—*choosing, prizing,* and *acting.*

4.   Use the decision-making process to assist you in your value judgments.

5.   Select a set of values that will give your life purpose and meaning.

6.   As much as possible, be guided by your values.

7.   Seek spiritual guidance from God.

The end of this chapter is like the beginning. Decisions, judging, value judgments are all yours to make. Your life will be lived in the context of your personal value judgments.

WHAT WOULD I DO?

"The Mailbox"

You just got off from your part-time job. It has been snowing and sleeting, and the streets are icy. You are going slow. Another car coming toward you begins to slide in your direction. To avoid hitting the car you jump a curb and crash into a mailbox, knocking it down. Nobody sees you. The other car does not stop.

What will you do?

Why?

What values are important to you in making your decision?

What other choices do you have?

What might be the results of your decision?

4

How Can I Cope with Change?

"I don't want to move to another city. It's unfair for you to take me from my friends." (Girl, 14.)

"I don't want to wear the same coat I wore last year. It's shorter than this year's dresses." (Girl, 16.)

"My dad used to play ball with me when he came home in the evening. Now he says he's too tired and just sits down and reads the paper." (Boy, 13.)

"My mom doesn't understand me at all. Why doesn't she change?" (Girl, 15.)

Ron is a seventeen-year-old. He is a junior in high school and actively involved in school athletics. He and Rhonda have had several dates. He has a car and a part-time job to pay for the car, the gas, and whatever it takes to keep the car running. Ron has a lot of friends. He enjoys going to his friends' homes and having them over to play pool at his house now and then. Ron is fairly active in his church. He sings, when work does not interfere, in the youth choir. He takes part in youth fellowships when he can.

Ron is happy with all the involvements he has except for one thing. The company his dad works for recently told Ron's dad that they would like to give him a promotion to vice-president of the company. This would mean a big pay raise and a big bonus immediately. There is one condition: He will be transferred to the home office, which is a thousand miles from where the family lives now.

What values are involved in making the decision to move? If Ron's dad takes the new position, what changes will take place for Ron? What adjustments will Ron have to make in his life? What would your reaction be to a change like this?

Kathy is a fifteen-year-old. She has two younger sisters, ages nine and eleven. About a year ago Kathy's mother found out she had cancer and died six months later. Kathy's father was very lonely and had difficulty adjusting to life without a wife. Kathy had to assume responsibility for much of the work her mother had always done. There was cooking, cleaning, shopping, and looking after younger sisters. While her father helped as much as he could and even hired out some of the work, the load on Kathy in addition to her schoolwork was tremendous.

How do you think these changes affected Kathy? What would your reaction have been?

These situations and the changes that resulted for these teenagers are repeated thousands of times every day in this country. These changes and others like them are very common. This chapter is about change and how you as a teenager can adjust to change.

Why Do Things Change?

Someone has said that nothing in life is certain except change. Things change. Between the time your parents were in high school and now, things have changed. In all probability you are taking courses in school that were not even offered when your parents were in school. Of course you are taking some that are the same, too. The following sections describe some familiar areas of change.

Fashions

You can check out how things change by looking at some old magazines or catalogs. Notice the difference in hairstyles, the way people dressed, the style of the cars. Even styles of houses have changed. If you are in high school, you may be able to remember the difference in the way you wear your hair now and the way you wore it in junior high. Or you may have noticed that the clothing you wore last year looks funny to you now because of the change in fashion in just one year's time.

Why do these things change? Why isn't a dress which you wore only a few times last year still OK to wear now? The answer to these questions is not a simple one. People's ideas about what they like may change. Advertising by merchants who make these things cause you to want new things different from the things you have now. You can think of other reasons why fashions change.

Customs

Other things change. Customs change. At one time people in a neighborhood could depend on living there for many years. Therefore, they became acquainted with their neighbors, entertained each other in their homes, and helped each other in times of difficulty. Because people move in and out of neighborhoods fairly quickly now, it is not unusual that a family will not even know their neighbors' names.

Values

There are many kinds of evidence that the values people hold are changing. Attitudes toward sex, toward divorce, and toward working mothers are examples of areas where values have changed very much. Many of the ideas that people once had about sex being bad and dirty have changed. Now many people see sex as a creation of God that is good and beautiful to be enjoyed within marriage. Views of sex as being OK outside of marriage are also evident.

Not too many years ago people who were divorced were thought of almost as outcasts. Mothers worked outside the home only when they had to help make money to support the family. Now divorce is more common and divorced people are more accepted. Many mothers have careers outside the home because they feel this is right for them.

Some of the ways values change are good; others are not so good. When a society's values change, the ways its people live and behave are affected. Your values guide your behavior. If your behavior changes but your values don't, you may feel guilty. If your values change, your behavior will also change. It is good to know what you value, what is important to you, and to follow this as a guide to life.

Careers

The kind of work that people do has changed greatly. The use of more and more machines to do more and more things has been partly responsible for this. To produce the kinds of goods and services that American people expect takes thousands of kinds of jobs. A person may change jobs and even career fields several times during his working years.

Educational emphasis has changed also. At one time it was thought that everyone should have a college education. There is a trend away from that idea. Technical and practical schools that teach a person a skill are very popular. Careers in entertainment and athletics challenge more and more young people.

In a later chapter of this book, you will read about work and setting life goals with regard to work. As you consider these, you will want to be aware of the effects of change now and in the future upon your own goals.

Families

Families change also. It may be that your family is made up of a mother, father, you, and your brothers and sisters. That kind of family has been the major kind in the past, but now it is not unusual to find a family made up of only one parent and the children. Some children find that they actually have two homes—perhaps their parents are divorced and each one remarried. Sometimes in a case like this the child spends part of the year with his mother and part of the year with his father.

Whatever the makeup of your family, you have had to adjust to changes in it during your life. Maybe you have experienced the birth of a new baby in your family. You may have had the experience of moving to a new location or the experience of having a grandparent coming to live with you. Perhaps an older brother or sister went away to college or got married. All these are examples of changes that might take place in a family. You may think of others.

People

Not only do families change, but people in those families change. Right now, you are going through many changes yourself. Physical, emotional (feeling), social, intellectual, and spiritual changes are all taking place. This is because you are growing and maturing. Adults change too. New jobs, additional education, and new friends are examples of things that can bring about change in adults.

There is change taking place all around you all the

time. You may not understand or like all the change you experience. There is change taking place in you and change that affects you, making you different.

How Does Change Affect You?

Change is not always comfortable. The changes that Ron and Kathy had to face, in the examples at the beginning of this chapter, are uncomfortable. Some teenagers facing changes of this kind become rebellious and resentful. Almost everything upsets them and makes them angry.

Ron, for example, may resent having to go to a new school, losing out on the athletic program, having to make new friends. He may feel that his dad is being grossly unfair to move the family at this important time in Ron's life. Kathy may be angry because she had to assume so much responsibility for her family. She may yell at her younger sisters and become upset if they do not help as much as she would like them to.

Your Personal Life

It is normal and natural to feel upset when a change brings about losses in your life. Ron experienced the loss of friends and status. Kathy experienced the loss of her mother and the loss of some of her personal freedom. If you continue to feel upset and angry for a long period of time, you may become physically ill. Or you may become an angry, resentful person who is ready to pounce on anything or anyone who does not do to suit you at all times.

Not all change is uncomfortable, of course. Sometimes change helps your feelings. Suppose one of your teachers announces a test for the next day. You already have plans for the evening and know you will not have enough time to properly prepare for the test. When you go to class the next day she announces that her plans have changed. The test will be next week. A change of that kind might be rather welcome. Some of the family changes that were mentioned earlier might bring joy and not be uncomfortable at all.

Some change brings about good and bad feelings at the same time. Ron may be uncomfortable about leaving his friends and at the same time excited about moving near mountains where he will be able to ski. In the example of the test being changed to a different day, a person who had studied very hard the night before might be angry to have the test postponed.

Change will have an effect upon you. To a certain extent you can choose how you will react to change and the kind of lasting effect it will have. It is just as easy to be angry, express your anger with words that say exactly how you feel, and then accept the change as a challenge to help you become a better person as it is to stay upset and angry.

Your Family Life

When one member of a family is upset and unhappy, everyone in the family is affected. The other members may not be as upset as the one member, but they are affected. Taking the opposite view, when one member is excited and happy about some change which has taken place in his life, other members will be affected also.

Because family members live close together and communicate with one another, usually on a daily basis, what affects one member affects all.

Again, a person usually has a choice about his reaction to change in himself. He has a choice about his reaction to change in other people. Ron can choose to be happy that his father received such a large promotion. He can try to understand how his dad feels about the promotion and the opportunities it will bring to him and the family. When a person really tries to see things from another person's point of view, it makes a difference in his reaction.

Teenagers, at times, have to try very hard to understand change from their parents' point of view. They sometimes have to understand it from their brothers' and sisters' point of view. It isn't always easy but will sometimes help make family life smoother.

Your Social Life

You have probably noticed many changes in your social life as you have grown up. When you were in elementary school your best friends were members of the same sex. You did not want to be with or near members of the opposite sex. This is generally the way young children respond. There are exceptions, of course.

As you have grown, however, members of the opposite sex have become more important to you. While you still value your friends of the same sex, you probably find yourself daydreaming about a member of the opposite sex. This is natural.

You will notice drastic changes in your social life as you go through the teen years. You will probably change from wanting many friends to valuing one or two close friends. You will probably spend hours with these closest friends listening to their hopes, dreams, and problems, and telling them yours.

You will lose friends from time to time. A friend will move away. You will attempt to write letters, call long distance, or even go to see that friend. After a while, however, you may find that all attempts to keep in touch tend to fail. You have new interests, and so does your friend. You may experience change in friendships simply because you and your friend decide that your friendship is not getting anywhere.

Through contacts at school and church, you may form new friendships. Friendships, social contacts, and boy-girl relationships seem to be in a state of change during these teen years. Sometimes the changes hurt. It is not easy to have your best friend move far away. It is painful to lose a boyfriend or a girl friend. Changes like these will be part of your experience during the teen years.

What effect will they have on you? To a great extent you are responsible for that. If you lose a friend you may decide that you will never get close to anyone else. You may decide that the risk of being hurt again is too great. Or you may decide to be glad that you had that person as a friend. A change in any aspect of your life will affect you, largely in the way you choose for it to.

How Can You Adjust to Change?

Much of life is uncertain. It has been pointed out that change is certain. Just what form the change takes and when is uncertain. Some change takes place gradually. Other change is sudden and unexpected. How can you cope with change? How can you plan for the future when you don't know what changes you will be facing? Should you just sit by and let change happen, or should you be active in helping to make changes?

Will Change Affect Your Future?

The answer is obviously yes. There is a challenge involved, however. Go back to the example of Ron. Ron had no way of knowing last year that his father would be promoted and transferred this year. The challenge that Ron faces is to understand and acknowledge the losses he feels, try to understand the new opportunities for his dad, and begin making plans for starting a new life in a new location. Before he moves, Ron might write for information about his new school. He might find out the possibilities for entering the athletic program. He might get information about part-time work. After he moves, he might start immediately attending a church. He might try to get acquainted with others who have just moved into the community. You may think of other things that would challenge Ron to make a good thing out of this family move rather than to continue to be miserable.

Can You Be Active in Making Change Happen?

Again the answer is yes. Some change occurs gradually and as a part of the process of living. For instance, the physical changes happening in your body are mostly beyond your control. Some change happens as a result of other events beyond our control. Suppose you are planning a ski trip during the Christmas vacation, but for some reason it does not snow in the mountains where you intend to go. Or suppose you plan to play golf on Saturday afternoon. When it rains, your plans have to be concelled. There are changes in the environment that you have little control over.

Some teenagers wish desperately that their parents would change. They think that their parents don't try hard enough to understand them or to listen to their point of view. This is sometimes true. Some parents do need to listen more carefully to their teenagers. However, it is also true that some teenagers could change their parents' reactions to them if the teenagers would make some changes. The chance of changing your parents is usually pretty small, so your best chance is to make some positive changes in you that your parents will notice. For example, if you want your parents to allow you to go more places with your friends, try emptying the trash without being told. Try helping clear the table after dinner without being told. Try cleaning your room and making your bed without being told. You might be surprised to find that more cooperative efforts on your part will bring some noticeable changes in your parents.

Do You Make Change or Does Change Make You?

In this chapter it has been shown that change affects you, but the permanent or lasting effects it has upon you are largely your choice. There are examples, of course, that tend to make us think that change makes us. Suppose a teenager is in a car wreck that leaves him paralyzed from the waist down. It is difficult to think that a change of this kind and the lasting effects it has are largely his choice. How can that be?

Remember the first chapter? The Whole You is affected when one part is affected. However, even if this teenager has physical paralysis, that means he still has a brain (an intellect). He still has emotions. Sure, he will be disappointed, resentful, and upset; but he doesn't have to stay that way. He still has friends. He still has life and can still worship God. What does all that mean? It can mean that even with the change he has experienced, there can be a challenge to make something of the changes.

Consider carefully the following statements about the effects of change upon you:

1. The way you adjust to change has something to do with your attitude toward the change.

2. Look for the choices you have. It may be that the change has given you a wider variety of choices.

3. Change brings your values into sharper focus. It makes those things which are important stand out and be useful to you.

4. It is not always possible to know just *what* change will take place or *when.* Sometimes you have time to anticipate a coming change and make plans for it.

5. If you have had some good experiences in adjusting to change when you were younger, those may help you in adjusting to change in the future.

6. Try to strengthen the things in your life that *probably* will not change. Family relationships are an example of this.

7. Sometimes you need to get in touch with someone who can help you adjust to your change. Your parents, a friend, your pastor, or a counselor are examples of people who may help.

A good way to summarize this entire chapter is to use this prayer: "God, grant me the serenity to accept the things I cannot change, courage to change the things I can, and wisdom to know the difference."

OPEN-ENDED STATEMENTS

"Changing"

Complete the following statements about what you would change if you could.

1. If I were my father I would _____
   _____.

2. If I were my mother I would _____
   _____.

3. If I were the mayor of my town I would _____
   _____.

4. If I were the principal of my school I would _____
   _____.

5. If I were to change one thing in my life I would ____
   _____.

6. If I could change where I live I would move to ____
   _____.

7. If I could change one thing in society I would _____
   _____.

PART II

VALUES AND CHRISTIAN COMMITMENT

5

What Can I Know About God?

"It's hard for me to understand God." (Teenage boy.)

"It seems that God is so far away." (Teenage girl.)

"What does God have to do with my values?" (Teenage boy.)

"Remember now thy Creator in the days of thy youth" (Eccl. 12:1.)

"I felt so young, so strong, so sure of God." (Elizabeth Barrett Browning.)

"If God be for us, who can be against us?" (Rom. 8:31.)

"At times I feel real close to God." (Teenage girl.)

You can tell from these statements that it is not a simple thing to know about God. One day you feel you are very near to God, the next far away. At times you seem to understand what God is all about. But something happens and then you are all mixed up. Maybe the following prayer helps explain some of your feelings.

Dear God

Dear God, I want you to know me.
   I want you to know where I hurt.
I want you to listen to my cries for help.
   I want you to listen to my heart concerns.
Dear God, I want you to help me.
   I want you to help me with my troubles.
I want you to understand me just as I am.
   I want you to understand me when I make mistakes.
Dear God, I want you to speak to me.
   I want you to tell me your will for my life.
I want you to love me just as I am.
   I want your help in loving you in return.
Dear God, I want you to always be with me.
   I never want to feel lonely again.
And please, God, I have other friends just like me.
   Would you give them the same blessing.

—Just a Youth

You are faced with many questions about God. You want to know who God is. You want to know why God made you. You want to know how you can relate to God. You want to know about God and your values. You also want to know how God affects your everyday life. The purpose of this chapter is to help you find beginning answers to these questions.

Who Is God?

God as Supreme Being

God has always existed. There has never been a time when God has not existed. God is the supreme being of the universe. As some anonymous writer wrote: "The world we inhabit must have had an origin; that origin must have consisted in a cause; that cause must have been intelligent; that intelligence must have been supreme; and that supreme, which always was and is supreme, we know by the name of God."

You, being a human, cannot fully define God, who is supreme. You remember the story of Moses approaching God at the burning bush (Ex. 3:1–22). God told Moses to go to the children of Israel and to tell them that God sent him. Moses asked God his name so he could tell the children of Israel who sent him. God answered Moses and said, "I am that I am." He told Moses to tell the people *"I am* hath sent . . . you" (Ex. 3:14).

What did that mean? God was telling Moses that he is the only God. As the only God, he has always existed. He exists now, and he will always exist. You see by this that God has always been. God as the supreme being of the universe has all power, all knowledge, and the ability to be everywhere with everybody through his Spirit.

God as Creator

God is not only a supreme being of the universe, but he is creator of heaven and earth. Look all around you and see the things that God has made.

What God Has Made

Flowers, fruits, and weeds
   Grains, grass, and trees
Plains, valleys, and mountains
   Creeks, rivers, and fountains
Bees, grasshoppers, and crickets
   Ants, spiders, and yellow jackets
Blue jays, sparrows, and hawks
   Geese, quail, and ducks

Whales, sharks, and red fish
   Trout, snapper, and catfish
Dogs, cats, and fox
   Horses, deer, and ox
Women, daughters, and mothers
   Men, brothers, and fathers—
    And God made them all.

      —*Carl Elder*

You can see the handiwork of God everywhere you go. God created the sun and moon and placed them in their exact location. Science says that if our sun were just a little closer, we would all burn up. And if it were just a little further away, we would all freeze to death. By this you can understand the God of creation. God doesn't botch things up. He does it right the first time. You can know who God is by accepting him as creator of all things.

God and His Providence

Another way you can understand God is to know about his providence. God keeps the universe in order. God set the exact rotation of our earth. God established the wind currents and ocean tides. God made seedtime and harvest.

God gave to man the ability to think. God made man in such a way that man has emotions. It has always been God's plan for man to take what God has made and use it wisely. By God's providence you are left to run your life the way you feel is right for you.

God doesn't break into your life and begin to run you like a robot. He wants you to make decisions. He wants you to come to know him as the only God. He wants you to know that he cares about you but accepts you as you are. By being under the protection of God you have assurance that this world will stand as long as God desires. And at the same time you have assurance that you can direct the affairs of your life toward a better knowledge of God or toward rejecting him. It is your decision.

Why Did God Make Me?

God always intended to make man and woman. God desired to make man and woman because he wanted a special creature made in his image. That means God so made you like himself that you have a mind to think; a will to act; emotions of love, hate, anger, mercy, laughter, crying, joy, sadness, compassion, and selfishness.

God made you with these special qualities. He also gave most of you the ability to see things, to taste things, to touch, to smell, and to hear.

Before you were born your father and mother fell in love with each other. They were married. This is God's way. God wants those who desire marriage to have their own mate.

So God let the natural process of conception and birth take place. You are a part of your parents, yet you are different from anyone else. Why? Because you are you. You have your own identity.

This identity of yours is the stamp of God upon your life. How? Because God did not make you to look like him. God made you a responsible, rational being with emotions and personality. God gave you the best part of himself—a mind, a will, and emotions.

In making you or permitting you to be born, God had a special reason. God wants you to have fellowship with him. He wants you to worship him. But God wants you to do this because you love him and you desire to worship him. You see, God wants you to know and accept his love and fellowship because you want it too. This is the reason God created you in such a special way. He desires fellowship with you through your worship, prayers, and service in his name. But he also wants you to have a say in directing your life.

How Can I Relate to God?

You can relate to God by believing that God is the creator of all things. Believing this, you next come to believe that God sent his Son, Jesus, to this world to make our hearts and souls right with God. You do this by faith. Your faith in Christ Jesus sets you free from sin and death. When you have taken this first step—accepting Christ as your personal Savior—a special relationship with God is completed.

By accepting Christ as Savior you became a part of the larger family of God known as Christians. The word *Christian* means those who follow Christ—his disciples. You then begin to relate to God as an obedient child. You pray to him. You worship him. You ask his guidance in the affairs of your life. You serve him by sharing your faith and concern for others.

You relate to God by making friends with other Christians. You can find other Christians at your school, your job, and your church. Being with others who love God will encourage you. You and your Christian friends will have opportunities to serve God together.

You can relate to God by studying his Word—the Bible. In the Bible you learn more about God and his purpose for your life. You learn the Bible principles God wants you to live by. That is, you learn how God wants you to live and act as a Christian.

You can relate to God by talking to him. That's what praying is—talking and listening to God's voice inside you. When you pray, tell God all the deep things of your heart. Tell God how you hurt and how you need answers to your problems. Tell God about your mistakes and ask his forgiveness. Listen to God as he gives to your heart and mind a sense of direction. Pray that you will want God's will to be done. Why? Because God knows what's best for his children. Earnest and sincere prayer is one of the best ways you can relate to God. Remember as you pray and ask God to do something that it may not be his will. But he will be with you as you work through each difficulty.

What About God and My Values?

God and Your Values

You have already learned that you acquire many of your values from your religius background. There are certain values that exist with God—that is, man did not make them. Some of the values that God has ordained (caused to be) are love, joy, faith, hope, patience, peace, gentleness, meekness, temperance, and goodness. You can find these values listed in Galatians 5:22–23. These are all God's values because they exist in his own nature in a perfect way. Paul referred to them as being "the fruit of the Spirit."

You also learned that values give a sense of direction for life. Your values help guide your behavior or conduct. God would have you to examine his values and see if you are willing to let them be your guide in life.

But Can I Choose My Own Values?

Yes, you can. That's why God gave you a will of your own. You can choose to live by God's values, or you can live by the world's values. There is a difference. For example:

God says give—the world says get.
God says love—the world says hate.
God says forgive—the world says get even.

God says peace—the world says war.

God says joy—the world says sadness.

God says goodness—the world says evil.

God says temperance—the world says eat, drink, and be merry.

God says faith—the world says there is no faith.

God says hope—the world says there is no hope.

It is up to you to make the choice of which value system you will live by—God's or the world's. Your ability to choose is why you are a very special creation of God. God wants you to decide by your own free will to accept his values to guide you through life.

Who Is Responsible for My Decisions?

You are. God has given you the ability to think through a situation before acting. God has made known to you certain basic values that will guide your life in the midst of any problem. Since you are a rational being and have the freedom of choice, you must accept responsibilty for your decisions—good or bad.

This ability to make your own decisions is why you are so unique. God desires that you live by his values because he already knows they are best for you. He wants you to find that out for yourself. He wants you to follow his principles of living because you want to.

There are at least three ways you can decide about accepting God's values for your life.

1. You can decide to accept God's values with a grudge—"I am forced to."

2. You can decide to accept God's values out of a sense of duty—"I ought to."

3. You can accept and live by God's values with thanksgiving—"I want to."

The first way you feel pressured. The second way you

feel a sense of obligation. The third way you feel that your decision comes from the heart. Not much will happen when you attempt to follow God's values with a grudge. A little more will take place in your life when you follow his values for duty's sake, but you will not have real joy in your heart. Deciding to accept God's values with thanksgiving opens up to your life real purpose and meaning. Still, you must decide. And whatever you decide, you are responsible for the results of your decisions.

How Can God Affect My Everyday Life?

He Is with You

When you are relating to God in a growing way, you feel his presence. God wants you to feel his presence. His nearness to you is a part of his nature. You can feel that God is a part of your everyday life. When you are at school, he is there. When you are at play, he is there. When you are at work, he is there. The sense of God's presence gives you strength and courage to make decisions that are right for you. In a real way God becomes your partner in your day-by-day living. The effect of this relationship on your life is best measured by you. Others will see a difference. But only you will know how deep it is in the heart.

He Influences You

You cannot feel God's constant presence without being under his influence. When you accept God, you accept his purpose to influence your life values. That is, you accept the fact that God will show you new ways to live. He will show you new ways to act. He will reveal to you new ways to serve others. His influence will always tug at your mind and heart.

You can be sure that his influence is good and perfect. He will show you the right way. He will show you the loving way. God's influence will always take you into consideration. God always acts for your welfare. He wants you to be a loving and happy person. He wants you to be maturing as you grow older. He influences you to desire the things that are right for you at each stage of your life.

He influences you to choose the right friends. God wants you to have friends who love him as you love him. You need friends you can trust. You need friends who are seeking to know more about God and his values for life. Your relationship with friends like that will help you to mature in your faith.

God Understands You

God affects your everyday life when you come to accept the truth that he understands you. God understands your problems, fears, emotions, desires, and growing pains. How does God do this? He knows these things about you because he made you in his image. He gave you life.

In having given you life, God wants you to have a productive life. He wants you to feel a sense of purpose. Even when you are faced with decisions or problems, God wants you to come to grips with them. He wants you to take what he has given you and act for the good of all—you and others.

Conclusion

Is it a good feeling to know God does understand and care? Is it a good feeling to know that he is always ready to hear you ask for help? Is it a good feeling to have a set of values—God's values—to guide you in life? Is it a good feeling that you are always under the influence of

God? Is it a good feeling that God gives you the freedom to choose? Are you glad you can relate to God? Are you happy that God permitted you to be born?

These are personal questions—questions that have been discussed in this chapter. You are the only one who can answer these questions for yourself.

WHAT WOULD YOU SAY?

"There Is No God"

You are standing in the hall at school with some friends, talking about your experiences in church the day before. Another friend, who never attends church, joins your group. He listens for a while and finally says, "You guys are wasting your time. There is no God."

How do you answer him?

What might be the results of your answer?

What other reasons could you give to convince him that God does exist?

Does your faith in God ever embarrass you? If so, why?

6

What Do I Know About the Church?

"My church is not friendly." (Teenage girl.)

"I really don't feel a part of my church." (Teenage boy.)

"My church has a good youth program." (Teenage girl.)

"Christ . . . loved the church, and gave himself for it." (Eph. 5:25.)

"Sometimes I just don't want to attend church." (Teenage boy.)

"The people make up the church, not the building." (Anonymous.)

"All I like about church is my choir." (Teenage girl.)

You can see from the above statements that different emotions and thoughts are expressed about the church. Have you ever asked yourself, "What do I know about the church?" You may not go to church at all and may know very little about the concept of church. You may go to church a lot and still confess you know very little about the church. You do know it is a place to worship.

You know the church is a place to study God's Word.

You know it is a place of various activities—religious and recreational. But what do you know about the deeper meaning of what the church is? Do you know who belongs to the church? Can you tell how the church affects your values? Do you know some of the values of your church? These questions deserve answers. This chapter seeks to help you with the answers.

What Is the Church?

Definition

Perhaps you were raised thinking the church was the building located at a certain place. You have heard people your age say, "I can't go; I'm going to church." Just about all your life you have thought the church was a place. Read the following that says something about what the church really is:

> The church is never a place, but always a people.
> The church is never a sacred building, but always
>   a believing assembly.
> The church is you who pray, not where you pray.
> A structure of brick or marble can no more be a church
>   than your jeans and shirt be you.
> There is in this world nothing sacred but man,
>   no sanctuary of God but the soul.
>
> *—Anonymous*

This statement raises two questions. First, what does the word *church* mean? And second, what is a definition of church? The word church in the original Greek language means the called out ones. This is referring to the Christians who were called to follow Christ and his teachings. They were called out of sin into a life of service for the Christ.

A simple definition is: The church is a body (people) of baptized believers in Jesus Christ banded together to do his work in the world until he comes again. There is the local church—that is, the local congregation. Then there is the larger concept that the church is made up of all believing Christians all over the world. Look at it this way. You worship with your church, God's people, in a building. At the same time many other people are doing the same thing all over the world. Just because it is impossible for all Christians to worship together at the same place and time doesn't change the fact that all are members of Christ's church.

Another way to grasp the meaning of the church local and the church universal is to remember when you are not at home with your family, you still belong to them. So it is with the church. You belong to Christ as a believer and attend church in your town. Other Christians whom you do not know are members of Christ's church and attend in their town. In both places believers have identified themselves with Christ. This brings up other questions that might help you know more about the church.

Who Formed the Church?

The Bible states that Jesus himself organized the church. He caused the church to be established by his own authority. He did this a long time ago. He told his disciples, "I will build [put together his people] my church; and the gates of hell shall not prevail against it" (Matt. 16:18).

What Is the Purpose of the Church?

Jesus had several things in mind when he told his disciples that he would establish his church. Perhaps the purposes listed below will give you some idea why Jesus organized the church.

Jesus established the church because:

1.   He wanted Christians to assemble and worship God together. We all serve the same God.

2.   He wanted Christians to cooperate together in spreading his teachings around the world.

3.   He wanted Christians to care for one another.

4.   He wanted Christians to encourage one another in the faith.

5.   He wanted Christians to meet together and study his word so they might be better disciples in the world.

6.   He wanted Christians to have the best possible human relationships—spiritually, socially, and emotionally.

7.   He wanted to establish his work of redemption among men.

8.   He wanted his followers to be identified with God—not the world.

9.   He wanted Christians to influence the world by their love, faith, and hope in the life hereafter.

10.   He wanted Christians to speak out against sin, wickedness, and immorality. Jesus wants you to live in the world but not as the world.

You can tell from this list that Christ's purpose in establishing his church was to allow us to grow spiritually and to praise and worship God.

Perhaps some of your questions about the church have been cleared up. Now look at the question, Who belongs to the church?

Who Belongs to the Church?

As you have already seen, the church is a different type of organization. It is not like a club. Clubs have restricted membership. Christ's church is open to all believers around the world. Many clubs require monthly or yearly payment of a fixed amount of money. Christ's church operates on freewill offerings called tithes and offerings. Clubs exist to glorify man. The church exists to glorify God. Think about the following questions.

What is church membership?

How do I become a member of the church?

What is my role in the church?

What Is Church Membership?

You need to understand two important things about church membership. *First,* when you become a disciple or follower of Jesus Christ, you are a member of his church right then. This is what is meant by the church universal—all of Christ's followers everywhere. *Second,* because you live in a certain place and because it is impossible for you to have fellowship with all Christians, you become a member of a group of Christians where you live. That is, you become a part of one of thousands of local congregations. You become a member of the local church.

There is yet another aspect of church membership. When you become a Christian and ask for membership in the local church, your name is added to the membership list. In this way the staff and members of the church can have contact with you. The next question deals with how you become a member of the church.

How Do I Become a Member of the Church?

You become a member of the church first by accepting Christ as your personal Savior. This means you come to believe by faith that Jesus is God's Son. You come to understand that sin—that which separates you from God—must be forgiven. That is exactly what Jesus does. He forgives your sin when you accept him as Savior. When this experience takes place in your life, you become a member of the church in the universal sense. You become a member of God's larger family of Christians who live around the world.

To become a member of a local congregation, you present yourself as a new Christian. You then are accepted into the local membership and you are baptized as commanded by Jesus. If you move to a new city, you will want to find a local congregation where you can continue to worship and serve God. Most local congregations will accept you on your statement as a Christian. Other churches will write to the church where you held membership for a letter of recommendation.

What Is My Role in the Church?

Let's suppose you are now a member of a local church. You are a new Christian. You may wonder just what your role in your church is. What can you do? How can you serve? Do you have a say in what programs are planned? You might even feel that you are not important to the church. Nothing could be further from the truth.

Every member of the church is important. You have a very special role to fill in your church—your own place. There are many ways you can feel a part of your church. Look at those listed below and put a check (√) next to each one you feel you could become involved in.

_____ 1. Member of a Youth Sunday School class.
_____ 2. Join the church youth choir.
_____ 3. Attend worship regularly.
_____ 4. Visit other youth for the church.
_____ 5. Attend special youth training classes.
_____ 6. Play on youth softball team.
_____ 7. Help clean up church property.
_____ 8. Participate in youth mission trip.
_____ 9. Help with Vacation Bible School.
_____ 10. Work in the bus ministry.
_____ 11. Serve on youth committee.

How many did you check? Maybe you checked just three or four. If you are faithful in just a few of these areas, you are finding your place in the church. As you grow older your role in the church will take different directions. For example, when you become a young adult you may find yourself teaching children or serving as a deacon. As you take part in the work and ministry of your church you learn more and more what the church is all about.

How Does the Church Affect My Values?

When you become a member of a local church fellowship, you represent that fellowship. You represent that fellowship and God to society around you. Your conduct, attitudes, and concerns reflect on your church—for good or bad. The church affects your values by making known to you God's values.

The church has certain values that are held up to the people. These values are generally shared with you in the pastor's sermons. They are taught to you through a Bible study class held at the church. The church is responsible to teach and preach these values that are found in God's Word. This is one of the main tasks of the church.

Values of the Church that Affect Your Values

Several basic values of the church tend to affect your values. Below you will find a list of some of these values. Read each value and place a check (√) by the ones you can accept.

_____ 1. God is one God.
_____ 2. Jesus Christ is the only Savior.
_____ 3. The church believes that man can have fellowship with God by and through the Holy Spirit.

_____ 4. God's supreme creation is man.

_____ 5. Man was created to love and worship God.

_____ 6. Human beings ought to love one another.

_____ 7. God is no respecter of persons.

_____ 8. Men ought to be temperate in all things.

_____ 9. All people should develop their minds and bodies.

_____ 10. Sexual experience between male and female should be reserved for marriage.

_____ 11. Drunkenness is to be avoided at all times.

_____ 12. Abuse of drugs is a sin against the body.

_____ 13. All earthly possessions are to be acquired through honest and honorable means.

_____ 14. All who can ought to work.

_____ 15. All people ought to love God and love neighbor as self.

_____ 16. All men ought to treat others as they would have others treat them.

_____ 17. Evil violence should not be tolerated among God's people.

Which ones did you check? Did you check them because you believe that they are right and that you *ought* to accept them? Or did you check them because these same values are your values too? That is, you attempt to live your life in such a way that these values are reflected in your conduct, work, attitudes, and concerns. If this is the case, then you can easily see how the church affects your values.

Through the church your moral values are influenced. The church influences your decisions about sex, drugs, honesty, drinking, and violence. The church influences your values and attitudes toward people of other races. The church influences your values in regard to your helping and caring about others. The church, through its many ministries, influences you to become concerned for the welfare of all mankind.

Because of the influence of the church, you have given to the hungry people of the world. Because of the influence of the church, you have helped others in many ways. You have found a way to serve God through your church. Perhaps while you read this page your church has influenced your life and values in such a way that you are committed to full-time Christian service. It is really hard to measure the influence of the church on the values and life of a youth who worships and attends regularly.

Conclusion

The church is a group of Christians. They generally have a place where they can meet together and worship God. By meeting together in worship and in studying God's Word, you are strengthened in your faith. This renewed strength permits you to serve God wherever you are.

As you attend and take an active part in the work and ministries of your church, your values and life are greatly influenced. You might feel that life has more joy and meaning. You find that through the church there are many ways that you can use your talents and abilities in service to God and man. You might find some of your own feelings about the church expressed in the following.

My Church

For my church, O God,
    I thank thee.
For thy people, O God,
    I thank thee.
They took me in
    when just a youth.
They helped me grow

to love thee, O God.
They did for me
 what the world could not.
They gave me a place
 to serve thee, O God,
They forgave my many
 mistakes, O God.
They changed my values,
 attitudes, and behavior.
They sought to prepare me
 for life's journey.
'Tis thy people I love
 in my church, O God.
They are my friends
 and I thank thee, O God,
For placing me in their midst.

     —Carl Elder

WHAT WOULD YOU SAY?

"What's in It for Me?"

You have just finished dressing for Sunday School and church. One of your friends calls and asks you to go to the lake with a group of your mutual friends. You state that you are going to church. She says to you, "What does church have for you? You are always going to church."

How do you answer her?

What might be the results of your answer?

What other reasons could you give her for wanting to attend church?

Does attending church have meaning for you?

7

How Can the Bible Affect Me?

"The Bible is too hard for me to understand." (Teenage boy.)

"Reading the Bible helps me when I feel down." (Teenage girl.)

"The Bible is God's chart for you to steer by." (Henry Ward Beecher.)

"I don't think my church teaches me how to understand the Bible." (Teenage boy.)

"Hold fast to the Bible as the anchor of your liberties; write its precepts in your hearts, and practice them in your lives." (Ulysses S. Grant.)

"I have just discovered the joy of reading my Bible." (Teenage girl.)

You can find all kinds of opinions about the Bible. All you have to do is ask people. Some say it is too hard to understand. Others say it is out of date. There are those who believe the Bible to be God's word to man. You must decide for yourself if you want to know more about the Bible. You must decide how you are going to let the Bible give meaning and purpose to your life. You alone will decide how the Bible will affect your values and behavior.

What Do I Know About the Bible?

What do I know about the Bible? This question has many answers. Some of the answers involve knowing how we got our Bible and who wrote it. Some of the answers involve knowing how the Bible is organized. It's important to know that the Bible is not one book but many. It is not one kind of literature but many kinds. Answers to the question also involve knowing how to find passages in the Bible which can help with different problems.

How Was the Bible Put Together?

In the early beginnings, God spoke his words to his prophets and they repeated his words to the people. Soon men who were gifted as scribes and could write their language well began to write on scrolls the words and commandments of God. They also wrote the early history of God's people.

The Old Testament was written in the Hebrew language and the New Testament in the Greek language. The various books (scrolls) of the Old Testament were put together first. These were placed in the Temple and referred to as Temple copies. The Temple copies were used to make other copies for other synagogues.

The various authors of the New Testament related to a scribe what God had revealed to them and what they had seen firsthand. These copies were sent to various Christian groups which in turn made other copies for their use.

The books of the Bible originally had no chapters or verses. The chapter divisions used today were made by Stephen Langton, archbishop of Canterbury, who died in 1228. Until the advent of the printing press, all versions of the Bible were handwritten. There were many different versions.

The first Bible printed by a printing press was the Gutenberg Bible of 1455. The King James Version, which is still one of the most popular versions, was translated from the original languages by order of King James of England. This version was completed and published in 1611.

Is the Bible the Word of God?

You must decide for yourself if you accept the Bible to be God's Word. There are many reasons which you might consider as you search for your decision.

1.   The Bible has stood the test of time.
2.   The Bible has stood the test of criticism.
3.   The Bible answers questions of history.
4.   The discovery of the Dead Sea Scrolls, containing large portions of Old Testament Scriptures, in 1947 has given additional validity to the Bible.
5.   The testimony of our Christian forefathers adds authenticity to the Bible.
6.   The testimony of Christians around the world gives validity to the Word of God.
7.   The account of ancient history indicates the authenticity of the Bible as the Word of God.
8.   The contents and concepts of the Bible suggest that it is the work of a supreme being.

These reasons and others may help you decide to accept the Bible as God's Word. One denomination has printed a statement of faith regarding the Bible. Can you accept the following statement for your own?

"The Holy Bible was written by men divinely inspired

and is the record of God's revelation of himself to man. It is a perfect treasure of divine instruction. It has God for its author, salvation for its end, and truth, without any mixture of error, for its matter. It reveals the principles by which God judges us; and therefore is, and will remain to the end of the world, the true center of Christian union, and the supreme standard by which all human conduct, creeds, and religious opinions should be tried. The criterion by which the Bible is to be interpreted is Jesus Christ."

Who Wrote the Bible?

Many different people wrote various books and sections of the Bible. We do not know how many people wrote the Bible. We do know there were more than forty. Some of the authors and their writings might be very familiar to you. Moses wrote some of the first five books of the Old Testament: Genesis, Exodus, Leviticus, Numbers, and Deuteronomy. Many other books of the Old Testament were written by the person bearing the name of a particular book. For example, the prophet Isaiah wrote the book of Isaiah and Daniel wrote the book of Daniel. The people who wrote the Old Testament wrote in Hebrew.

The authors of the New Testament books are more familiar than some of those of the Old Testament. These books were written in Greek. Matthew, Mark, Luke, and John were written by disciples of Christ and were known by these same names.

The apostle Paul wrote more books of the New Testament than any other author. Some of the books Paul wrote are Romans, 1 and 2 Corinthians, Galatians, Ephesians, Philippians, and Colossians. Books Paul wrote are often called epistles. They were short letters to different Christian groups.

A Bible dictionary or a Bible commentary will help you know about authors of other books.

We do not know all of the authors of the Bible. We do know that all of the authors of the Bible acted under the authority of God. It is because of their faithfulness to write down God's revelation of himself to man that the Bible has been preserved until this day.

How Is the Bible Organized?

The Bible is divided into the Old Testament with thirty-nine books and the New Testament with twenty-seven books. The Old Testament has seventeen historical books including the five books of law, five poetical books, and seventeen prophetic books. The New Testament is divided into the four Gospels, one historical book, twenty-one epistles, and one book of prophecy. Look in a Bible dictionary or guidebook to find the books that belong in each category.

What Meaning Does the Bible Have for My Life?

You may find on reading the Bible that it will speak to many of your needs. The Bible tells you how to make peace with God. The Bible tells you how your life can have meaning and purpose, and it helps you face the realities of everyday living. The Bible helps you relate to others in a caring way. The Bible gives guidance when you are sad, lonely, or discouraged.

The Bible tells you about God and his will among men. It tells you about salvation in Jesus Christ. The Bible speaks of heaven for those who believe in Christ and a hell for those who reject Christ. The Bible tells you that God loves you and that God showed this love when he sent Jesus to this earth to die for your sins.

You can find meaning for your life by reading the Bible

when you are confronted with life's difficulties and problems.

The following list suggests some specific problems and passages to read.

—In sorrow, read John 14
—In danger, read Psalm 91
—If God seems distant, read Psalm 139
—When discouraged, read Isaiah 40
—If faith fails, read Hebrews 11
—You are "blue," read Psalm 34
—You need companionship, read Psalm 23
—You are worried, read Matthew 6:19–34
—You need forgiveness, read Psalm 51
—Life seems empty, read John 15
—You feel cheated, read Psalm 103
—Friends fail you, read Psalm 27
—You are sleepless, read Psalm 4:4–8
—You are bored, read Psalm 104:23–24; 33–34
—You are jealous, read James 3:13–18
—You are angry, read Matthew 5:9,22

As you come to accept the Bible as God's word to man about salvation and redemption through Jesus Christ, you will also discover its meaning for everyday life. You will find it to be your guide. It will give you a sense of direction. You will find joy and strength within its pages. You will find help as you ask God how you are to use your life.

How Can the Bible Affect My Values?

Your values guide your actions and thoughts as you live day to day. You get your values from family, religion, and society.

The Bible has a great deal to say about your values. The degree to which the Bible affects your values depends largely on your personal commitment to its teachings. To illustrate this there are ten basic human values listed on the left and a Scripture quotation listed to the right of each value. As you study the list, decide if the Bible has affected the way you live in these ten areas. If it has, then you can say the Bible does affect your values.

Love	"Love one another" (John 15:17).
Kindness	"Be ye kind one to another" (Eph. 4:32).
Faith	"The just shall live by faith" (Heb. 10:38).
Wealth	"Take heed, . . . for a man's life consisteth not in the abundance of things which he possesseth" (Luke 12:15).
Power	"All power is given unto me in heaven and in earth" (Matt. 28:18).
Honesty	"Provide things honest in the sight of all men" (Rom. 12:17).
Respect for all men	"Honour all men. Love the brotherhood. Fear God. Honour the king" (1 Pet. 2:17).
Patience	"The trying of your faith worketh patience" (Jas. 1:3).
Forgiveness	"Forgiving one another, even as God for Christ's sake hath forgiven you" (Eph. 4:32).
Work	"But rather let him labour, working with his hands the thing which is good" (Eph. 4:28).

How Can the Bible Affect My Behavior?

As you choose to let the Bible affect your values, you will also make the choice to let it affect your behavior. You may say that you hold certain values that are taught in the Bible, but in your daily behavior there are some obvious conflicts. It is one thing for you to accept a certain value. It is another for you to live out that value in your life's actions and decisions.

For example, you say you believe the Bible teaches you that you should care for your body. That's good. But in your daily life you do not get enough sleep, you smoke and drink, you abuse drugs, and you treat your body badly. If this is true, then the Bible has not affected your behavior in caring for your body.

Believing in something—a value of principle—that truly affects your life must become a part of your behavior. You must decide to do something with the value. Put it into action. Let the value become a part of your behavior as seen by family, friends, and society.

The Bible is a guidebook for you to use in evaluating your behavior. You need to experience the feeling every day that your behavior is in line with what you value, that your overall behavior is also in line with what God says is right for you. Who determines this? You do. You must live your own life. You must evaluate your own behavior.

Conclusion

The Bible affects many people all over the world. Most people who read and study the Bible are affected in positive ways. You will choose for yourself if you will take time to study the Bible and see what it has to say to you. You alone will let it affect your values and behavior by discovering for yourself its meaning and purpose. The task will last all your life because time and time again you will turn to the Bible for help and direction.

WHAT WOULD YOU DO?

"Bible in My Hands"

It is 9:00 P.M. on Saturday night. You have just gone to your room and picked up your Bible to begin studying for a part you said you will give in the Senior High Sunday School department the next morning. You sit down and the phone rings. It is for you. Your friend Tom asks you to go to a late show with him.

What will you do?

Why?

What might be the results of your choice?

What other choices do you have?

8

What Does Christian Love Mean to Me?

"Being loved by my family is very important to me." (Teenage girl.)

"Sometimes I feel as if nobody loves me at all." (Teenage boy.)

"Knowing that God loves me makes a difference in my life." (Teenage girl.)

"Love is an image of God, and not a lifeless image, but the living essence of the divine nature which beams full of all goodness." (Martin Luther.)

"These things I command you, that ye love one another." (John 15:17.)

"I don't want a lot of things. I just want to feel that I am loved just like I am." (Older teenager.)

Love has just as many definitions as there are people. To you love means one thing; to your friend it means another. You might feel that to love means to hug and to kiss. Or you might think that love is caring for others. You can tell from the above statements that real love is a necessity of all mankind. You need love. Everybody needs love. That's the way God has made us—a people who need love and need to give love. This chapter seeks to discuss the meaning of Christian love. Therefore, the sexual and romantic aspects of love will not be discussed.

What Is Christian Love?

What is Christian love to you? Is it loving as Christ loves? Is it just a deep concern for others? Does Christian love include service to others? Perhaps the following statements can start your thinking on what Christian love is to you.

Christian Love Is—
—loving God with all your heart.
—loving Christ, your Savior.
—loving your neighbor as yourself.
—loving your enemies.
—sharing with others.
—caring for others.
—weeping with others.
—rejoicing with others.
—helping others.
—doing for others.
—kind and patient.
—not envious of others.
—not puffed up.
—always seeking the truth.
—God in you.
—you in God.

It is impossible to give a complete definition of Christian love. The only way you could do this would be to give a full account of the origin and mind of God. Not one person in our world could do that. Christian love is many things to many people. As you read the following maybe you can add to the list.

Christian love is accepting love from God.   Before you can love in the Christian sense, you must receive love— God's love. Above all else that is true in this world is the fact that *God loves you.* He loves you just as you are. He loves you and wants you to love him. He wants you to receive his love as shown to you through his Son, Jesus.

Christian love is a gift.   If you are ever going to have Christian love, then you must be willing to receive it from God as a gift. It's free! You can't work for it. You can't bargain for it. You can't live a good enough life to earn it. God's love is free to all who believe.

Christian love is loving God.   How can you love God when you have rejected his love for you? You can't. When you accept Christ as Savior, you accept by faith all the love God has for you. You start loving God right then. You grow in the love as you learn more about God. Your love for good matures as you continue to serve him through his church.

Christian love is following Christ's teaching. Christian love brings a challenge to your life. It is not a simple thing to live under the challenge of Christian love every day. There are conditions to your accepting God's love. Jesus was God's spokesman. Jesus said, "If ye love me, keep my commandments" (John 14:15). You can see that one major aspect of Christian love is to follow the teachings of Christ. You begin to see that love—God's kind of love—costs you something.

Christian love is doing for others.   What experience have you had that gave you the most inward joy? Was it a certain pleasure you participated in? Was it something you accomplished in school? Was it something you made? Or was it something that you did for somebody else with no thought of even a thank you in return? You did it out of love. It was the right thing to do. You did not think of yourself. That is Christian love.

Christian love is loving others. Do you love everybody? Do you love everyone God loves? Do you love those who don't speak to you as you walk down the halls at school? Do you love those who seem to make an effort to shun you at church? Do you love the "creeps" who sell and abuse drugs? Do you love those who seem to dislike you? How would you react to the following story?

Dirty Sam

"Dear Lord, I got a problem. I just can't bring myself to love Sam. He is so dirty. His clothes are dirty. His hair is dirty. His body is dirty. And another thing, he has the dirtiest mouth. He tells nasty jokes. He swears all the time. Why don't you just take him away? When I see him coming, I turn away so he won't see me. I know I should try to love Sam. I know you love him even though he says he doesn't want anything to do with you. Dear Lord, what am I going to do? I am really mixed up."

Do you know a Sam? Are you still trying to love him because you know God wants you to? Are you trying to love him because, whatever he is, he is a human being? Perhaps your love and concern could help your Sam change. This kind of Christian love is hard. You must not just love Sam in the Lord, but you must will to love Sam yourself. You pay a price for this kind of love. But this kind of love gets at the real meaning of Christian love.

What Are Some Christian Principles of Love?

As you read the Bible carefully, you will begin to see some basic principles of love. You must decide if you want to accept these principles. You decide if you want to make them become a part of your relationship with God, self, and others. It will not be an easy task. The Christian way of love takes faith in God and deep personal commitment. Learning to love as God loves will take all your life, and even at life's end you will be still growing in his love. There are six principles of Christian love that you might consider accepting for yourself.

Love God with all your heart. This is the first commandment. You need to know that you must first love God before you can truly love anybody else. This means you love what God loves. God loves his son, Jesus—you must love him too. God loves all people—you must love them too. God loves his creation—you must love it too. Loving God as Lord and Savior means loving him with your whole being—heart, mind, and soul. When you come to the place in life that you can honestly say, "I love God with all my heart, mind, and soul," you are then ready to begin the journey of experiencing Christian love.

Respect yourself. To respect yourself you must love yourself. The best way to know that you love yourself is to feel good on the inside. You can best feel good on the inside by living, acting, and loving in ways that are right for you. Your attitudes, values, and behavior determine how much you love and respect yourself. If you live contrary to what you believe and what you know is right, you will soon lose respect for yourself. When you lose respect for yourself, you cease to love yourself. A vast empty space grows inside you with very few happy experiences. But it doesn't have to be that way. You alone will decide which way it will be with you.

Go the second mile. You will find as you grow older that the principle of Christian love is difficult at times. Going the second mile means the real Christian love does not seek the easy way out. You will be asked to do something for someone you love. Your love for him will see you through to the end of the deed. Love doesn't give out in the middle of the struggle—it keeps on going. This kind of love sent Jesus all the way to the cross.

Love keeps on forgiving.   Someone causes you a great deal of trouble or pain. Your love forgives him. In a short time he does the same thing again—your love forgives him. Why? If you can't forgive him, resentment will build up. Finally your relationship with God will suffer. Why? God will forgive him of his wrong just as he forgives you of your wrong. God will do this every time you ask. It is God's principle of loving you, and he wants you to "pass it on."

Seek what is right.   That's the way of Christian love. Always seeking what's right. Always seeking the truth. Your love for others will show openly when you seek their best welfare. The Bible says, "Therefore, all things whatsoever you would that men should do to you, do you even so to them: for this is the law and the prophets" (Matt. 7:12). Living by this principle of Christian love helps in your relationships with others. You come to acquire a life-style that seeks the right way because that's the way of love.

Love your enemies.   This will be the hardest test of your Christian love. It is easy to love those who love you. But the real test of Christian love is to love someone who is your enemy. You are not to love his evil ways, but him as a person whom God loves and cares about. To love someone who has said he hates you is indeed a hard thing. You will struggle with this. But if you begin to hate, then you become just as they are. You alone will decide to let God help you grow in this aspect of Christian love. Do you have an enemy? If you do, start loving him and see how long he remains your enemy.

Not one of these principles is to be taken lightly. You will find yourself loving God and everybody one day and the next fighting down your hate for someone. No person, except Jesus, can completely live by these Christian principles of love. You can accept them—that's your choice. You can put them into action in your life. That's your choice also. If you do practice the quality of love as set forth in these principles, your life will experience a real inward joy and peace.

How Does Christian Love Affect My Values?

Your understanding and living by the principles of Christian love will affect your values in the following ways:

Value of self. Loving yourself—having self-respect— will cause you to take care of your body. You will desire to train your body and mind to become what God intends for you to become.

Value of others. Your love for others will affect your attitude and relationship. You will seek their best interests and not your own.

Personal values. Your personal values such as honesty, kindness, cleanness, respect, and integrity will be motivated and influenced by love and not by selfishness. Love will help you make the right personal decisions in difficult moral situations. Love will help you decide what's best for you—not what you desire. God's kind of love colors your whole life. Living by his principles of Christian love affects all your values and all your decisions.

Economic values. Loving the way God wants you to love gives you a different outlook on possessions and wealth. You soon find out that possessing a lot of things such as a car, TV, stereo, money, and even knowledge is not as important to you as loving God, yourself, and your friends. You give love and you get love in return. You cannot get love from things. Christian love helps you understand that it is more blessed to give than to receive.

Society's values. Love helps you test the values of society. You test society's values against the principles of love. In doing so you will be able to decide what values of society are acceptable to you. You can then discard those that do not measure up to the principles of love. For example, society accepts smoking and drinking as a lifestyle. But you decide, because of love for your body, to reject them. The principle of love has overruled the principle of pleasure. Why? Because you willed it that way. It was your choice.

How Does Love Affect My Relationship with Others?

Have you come to the place in your Christian life that you can honestly say you love everybody as God loves them? If you have, then that kind of love will give a positive effect to your relationships with others. You will find yourself thinking the best of other people, particularly your friends. You will find that love will motivate you to speak kindly of your friends. You will have opportunities to help others.

Growing in Christian love can help you guard against many of the negative attitudes and emotions of interpersonal relationships. Some of these are as follows:

Envy—wanting what others have or wanting to be like somebody else.

Jealousy—envy; resentment against a friend or friends.

Gossip—talk about the affairs of others that puts them down.

Anger—always showing anger or resentment toward others.

Rejection—putting people down. Refusing to make friends or to speak to certain people.

Accusing—always blaming others for your troubles and problems.

All of these are strong negative attitudes and emotions that will block your relationships with others. A strong desire on your part to follow the principles of Christian love will help you maintain wholesome relationships with others.

Conclusion

This chapter has sought to help you understand what is involved in Christian love. You need to know what Christian love is. You need to experience it. You have looked at the principles of Christian love. You will decide if you follow them. You saw how love can affect your values. Again, you must decide if you want Christian love to be your foundational value. As you read chapter 9, "How Do I Get Along With Others?" maybe you will conclude that Christian love must be first in all your dealings with others.

WHAT WOULD YOU DO?

"Changed Plans"

You just accepted a date to go to the movies and dinner on Saturday night. At 6:00 P.M. on Saturday your girl friend calls and tells you that her mother and father have been in a serious accident and asks you to go to the hospital with her. She is crying as she tells you. Do you cancel your date?

What will you do?

Why?

What other choices do you have?

What might be the consequences of your choice?

What is the loving thing to do in this situation?

PART III

LIVING WITH MY VALUES

9

How Do I Get Along with Others?

"I wish I had more friends." (Girl, 14.)

"My mother and I can't seem to get along at all any more." (Girl, 16.)

"My parents don't understand me and I don't understand them." (Boy, 17.)

"My friends want me to do things that I don't want to do. How can I refuse and still have them for friends?" (Boy, 15.)

"To have a friend, one must be a friend." (Anonymous.)

You may have had some of these same problems or other problems in relating to others. This chapter is a discussion of how you can effectively relate to others. It covers areas such as how your values affect your relationships, how your self-image affects your relationships, and ingredients of effective relationships. Each person needs other people in order to be a person himself. Learning to form friendships and to make relationships better with family and friends is an important lifelong task.

You and Your Self-Image

From the time you were born, you have been developing a self-image (a picture in your mind of the way you are). The picture you have formed is a result of the many experiences you have had and your reactions to these experiences. Every time you have succeeded at something, you may have reacted in a positive way and told yourself you were a worthwhile person. Or you may have reacted in a negative way, telling yourself that it could have been better. When other people tell you things about yourself, this helps you form the picture you have of yourself as a person.

What you think of yourself as a person will have something to do with the ways you relate to other people. If you tend to think positively about yourself most of the time, you are then able to think positively about other people. If you have a negative opinion of yourself most of the time, you will tend to have negative attitudes toward others.

A positive self-image or self-concept is one of the most valuable things you can possess as a person. Being positive about yourself does not mean being a bragger or a boaster. It does not mean that you feel better than others. It does not mean that you put down others or feel conceited.

Having a positive self-image means that you are in tune with yourself as a person. You recognize and feel good about doing something well. You recognize areas in which you need improvement. You recognize a failure but use it as a means for learning. You recognize that sometimes others will do things better than you do, but other times you will do things better.

You recognize that at times people will say things to put you down. This does not mean that the things they say are true. If you have a positive self-image, you decide whether the statements are true. If they are, you can then choose to change for the better. If the statements are not true, you can decide that the statements were the other person's problem—not yours. As you think about your relationship to others, think about your own image of yourself.

How Do Your Values Affect Your Relationship to Others?

Of all the human values, the one chosen by most people as being the most important is affection or love. This means that the most important thing in life to most people is to be loved and to love.

The Development of the Value of Love

Nothing affects life more than the presence or absence of love. When a baby is born, it needs food, water, and protection from cold or heat. Those things are important for its survival. But if a baby is to develop as a person and develop a personality, it must have contact with another human.

The baby must have someone to hold him, talk to him, handle him, caress him, and love him. These are the kinds of things that help a baby grow into an individual who has worthwhile feelings about himself. Without being held, caressed, and loved, the baby does not learn how to be a person.

As the baby grows, he needs someone who will talk to him. He continues to need holding and caressing. He also needs guidance and protection from danger until he learns little by little to protect himself. From this kind of care a baby learns to relate to other people and to love other people. He first learns love by being loved and loving his parents. Then he learns to love others in his life who help make it a safe world for him to live in.

Although you were not aware of this happening to you as you grew, your early experiences have helped to form your ideas of love. As you grew you gradually learned to love not only your parents, your brothers and sisters, and grandparents, but your teachers, playmates, and friends. Eventually, you may learn to love a member of the opposite sex enough to want to live with her or him the rest of your life.

The Definition of Love in a Relationship

Love and affection are very much a part of your life and have been since you were a baby. There are many definitions of love. Love usually includes warm feelings that you have toward another person. It generally means that you want what is best for the other person more than you want that for yourself.

Love for a person can grow as you get to know that person. You may have had the experience of meeting someone and not being sure whether you liked that person. As you got to know him you began to like him and realized that he was really an important person in your life. Love for another person is sometimes based on how much you like that person. If you have many interests in common and can share your feelings freely with each other, this is a good basis for a loving relationship to develop.

Expressions of Love in a Relationship

Love can be expressed between members of the same sex as well as between members of the opposite sex. Think of all the people you love. You love your mother, your father, your bothers, and sisters. You probably also have at least one or two other adults in your life whom you love. You also have friends with whom you share your deepest feelings. Although you might not say "I love you" to these friends, you have loving feelings for them.

Love in a relationship can be expressed in a number of positive ways. Some people value touching as a way of expressing love and affection. This can be done by a warm, friendly handshake or a gentle, loving pat on the back or arm. Just taking someone's hand into yours and holding it gently can be an expression of love. Other people value expressions of love such as the doing of kind deeds. Helping your parents with things that need to be done around the house without having to be made to do so is an expression of love. There are countless actions that express the affection you feel for another person.

Words are nice too. A simple "I love you" spoken with gentleness and caring can mean so much to that person. Words, however, can also be very empty unless there are actions to back them up. To tell someone you love him and at the same time show unkindness in any way is an empty expression of love.

The ultimate expression of love and affection between members of the opposite sex is sexual intercourse. This is reserved for someone who is very special and can be best expressed between husband and wife. As you grow and mature, you will learn to value this expression of love highly. Understanding the value it can have for you and for another person takes waiting and maturing.

Many times a person will use the love he has for another person as a tool to get his own way. How many times have you thought or even said, "If you loved me, you would let me have my way." Or the opposite statement goes, "You must let me have my way or I will not love you."

Either of these points of view is an attempt to control or manipulate another person with love. Parents and children sometimes get into this kind of power struggle.

Also, friends sometimes try to use or manipulate each other by withholding or giving love in exchange for having their way. Real love is given and received unconditionally. Relationships with others that are based on genuine love make up the highest form of relationships.

Special Problems in Relating to Others

Power

One problem in relating to others is the problem of power. That was mentioned briefly in the last section. When a relationship is based on power, that means that one person feels a need to always have his way; and he expects others to always give him his way. No doubt you have known people like this. It is difficult for this kind of person to have many lasting friendships. He may have some friends; but when these friends get tired of always giving in to him, they desert him for other friends.

Usually a person who wants power over another really does not like himself too well. His self-concept is poor. He may brag a lot and be a bully, but he is probably really shy and afraid of other people. He is probably fearful that people will not like him, so he tries to make them like him by being forceful. Of course, this only causes more problems for him.

Value Conflicts

A special problem in relating to others develops when your values are in conflict with the other person's. A girl, for instance, may value her sexuality and desire to save sexual intercourse until she is married. Perhaps her boyfriend values his sexuality but does not understand why he must wait until marriage to have intercourse. This value conflict can cause problems in a relationship.

You may value your decision not to smoke cigarettes

or pot or not to drink alcoholic beverages. Your friends, however, may value doing these things as signs of being grown-up—of having entered into the adult world. If you continue to have these friends, you may have to choose between your values and theirs. Or you may have to choose between their friendship and your own values. In value conflicts the choice is yours. The decisions are not easy to make and sometimes cause problems among friends. Being true to your own values usually pays off in the end.

Prejudice

Another problem in relating to people is prejudice. Prejudice means making a prejudgment about a person or group without getting to know the person or groups first. Prejudice affects relationships with others. If you have a negative opinion of people with red hair, for example, you have prejudged all persons with red hair.

So if you are introduced to a person with red hair, you may say to yourself, "I don't like this person because he has red hair." When you do this, you do not give yourself a chance to become acquainted and find out for yourself just what kind of person the individual is. This is only one example of how a prejudice might affect relationships.

Prejudices are quite common. However, when you form prejudgments of individuals or groups without the benefit of acquaintanceship or relationship, you may deprive yourself of some valuable friendships.

Confidentiality

Still another problem in relating to others is confidentiality. That is a pretty big word, and it can be a pretty big thing among friends. If one of your friends tells you something and says, "Please don't tell this to anyone," your friend is asking you to be confidential. He is taking you into his confidence. He is asking you to keep a secret. If you tell someone else, you have broken the confidence. And the friend will know that you cannot be trusted with his deep feelings.

Confidentiality is an important ingredient in friendship. Friends enjoy sharing their deep feelings with each other. In order to have people share things with you, they must know for sure that you will not tell all your other friends. If you have difficulty in keeping confidences, it would be better for you to tell your friends ahead of time that you would rather not have them tell you things that are confidential. Repeating a confidence to others destroys trust, and trust is a basic ingredient of true friendship.

You may have had the experience of telling someone something which you did not want told to anyone else. When you found out that the person did tell another and that your secret was out, you felt very hurt. A guide to whether or not to tell someone something that someone else told you is to ask yourself, "How would I feel if this were told about me?" This brings up the discussion of putting yourself in someone else's place. This will be discussed in the following section.

Ingredients of Effective Relationships

Empathy

What does it take to relate to people in a way that will be satisfactory to both persons? One necessary ingredient of friendships and relationships of any kind is *empathy*. In the previous section mention was made of the ability to put yourself in someone else's place. "Feeling with" another person is a definition of empathy. When you have empathy for another person, you are able to see things almost the same way he sees them. You are able to put yourself in the center of his world and experience the things he is experiencing in the way he is experiencing them.

A few examples of how this works in relationships may help. Suppose your mom has spent a lot of time and effort cleaning the house and getting it just right. You come home from school, put your books on the dining table, deposit your shoes in the den, and have a snack in the kitchen, leaving snack dishes, crumbs, and various other things around. Your mom returns home from grocery shopping, surveys the situation, and becomes upset. From *your* point of view, she may be unreasonable. After all, isn't it her place to clean house and pick up after the family? Isn't that all she has to do all day?

If you have empathy for your mom, you will look at things from her point of view. You may respond to her comments with something like, "Gee, Mom, the house does look nice. You must have spent a lot of time on it. I was thoughtless to make a mess of it and leave my things out." A comment like this saves an uproar and may even bring back a reply from Mom such as, "I'm sorry. I am a little tired from cleaning and grocery shopping. Please just try to be more careful next time." End of discussion.

Another example of empathy might take place between two friends. Consider the following conversation between two friends:

"Hi, Mike."

"Hello, Jim."

"I am really upset, Mike. I had a date with Jill tonight, and she called and canceled it."

"Gosh, Jim, I'm sorry. Did she tell you why?"

"No, she just said she couldn't go tonight. And when I asked her for next week, she said she couldn't go then either. I really feel low. I don't know what is wrong."

"You really are feeling bad because you were counting on her going with you tonight."

"Yeah. I had everything planned and even had permission to drive my dad's car. I'm really angry."

This short conversation illustrates a friend being empathic and helpful to another person who is upset.

Listening

In the conversation in the preceding section, notice how Mike listened to Jim. Listening is a very important part of empathy and an ingredient of effective relationships. Notice how Mike responded after he had heard what Jim said. Notice that he did not respond with some cute or sarcastic comment such as in the following conversation:

"I am really upset, Mike. I had a date with Jill tonight but she called and canceled it."

"How come you to ask Jill for a date, anyway? You know she's the most popular girl at school. You think she'd really go with you?"

This sort of reply is a real turnoff. Not only will it keep Jim from continuing this conversation with his friend; it will keep Jim from expressing his feelings to his friend Mike again. It may even end the friendship.

Respect

Besides empathy and listening, another ingredient of an effective relationship is a feeling that others are equal with you and you are equal with others. Earlier in this chapter, you read about how important a good self-image is. It is important to feel good about yourself so that you can also feel good about others. As you become aware of your own feelings (emotions), you can also become aware that other people have feelings, too. You become aware that what makes you happy may not affect your friend in the same way. People respond differently to the same situations. Knowing this helps you realize that whatever a person feels is OK. Your friend does not have to feel the same way you do about something. It is important to know what a person feels is *real* to him.

Realness

Being real and not phony is an important ingredient in relationships. Faking concern or love for others causes you to feel bad. You may be able to fool others for a little while; however, they will soon catch on to your real feelings. This does not mean that you have to always reveal your *real* feelings, either positive or negative, about others. It sometimes helps to keep your feelings to yourself. At the same time it is good for you to understand what your true feelings are and ask yourself questions such as:

"What is there about me that causes me to respond negatively or positively to that person?"

"Which of my values—love, power, or control—is affecting this friendship?"

You will not like everyone, and everyone will not like you. This does not mean that you are a failure or not a worthwhile person. That is simply the way things are. As you learn some of the basic ingredients of friendship and relationship and begin to use them, you may notice a change in the way others respond to you. It is important to remember that you cannot change other people. You can change yourself, and that may result in changes in others also.

Conclusion

At the beginning of this chapter you read the statement "To have a friend, one must be a friend." That is a good summary of the things that have been talked about here. In forming friendships, there is nothing that really takes the place of a genuine concern and caring for others. In strengthening relationships with family and friends, caring and concern are also important. Relating well to others takes a willingness to be a friend and a willingness to do your part to have a good relationship.

WHAT WOULD YOU DO?

"Girl Problems"

You are about to get in your car at school when one of your friends stops you and begins to accuse you of taking his girl. He says he does not want you to date her. He also implies that friends do not do things like that. He is really upset with you—even angry.

What will you do?

Why?

What other choices do you have?

What might be the results of your decision?

How can you restore your friendship?

10

How Do Values Affect My Citizenship?

"I am only fifteen. How can I make changes in my government?" (Teenage girl.)

"I just turned eighteen, and I finally get to vote." (Young man.)

"How can teenagers be good citizens when we read in the papers about men in government being dishonest?" (Teenage boy.)

"My country has its faults, but I don't want to live any place else but America." (Teenage girl.)

"I'm just in the seventh grade. How can I help my country?" (Boy, 12.)

"No free government, or the blessings of liberty can be preserved to any people but by a firm adherence to justice, moderation, temperance, frugality and virtue." (Patrick Henry.)

Even though you are young, you can tell from the above statements that some youth are concerned about their government. Have you ever thought about the fact that you are a citizen? Do you know how your values affect your citizenship? Do you have a basic knowledge of your government? Have you ever felt like taking part in government affairs? Can you have a part in changing government laws, decisions, and methods? These questions are what this chapter is all about.

Am I a Citizen?

As a citizen, you are a member of a city, state, or nation. As an American citizen you are a citizen of your own town, the state you live in, and the United States. You are subject to the rights and responsibilities of all citizens. Your government protects your rights, and it is your decision if you are to be loyal in return.

You are a citizen if you were born to parents who are citizens. You are a citizen even though you were born elsewhere in the world just as long as your parents are citizens. Suppose your parents are missionaries or in the military service in another country; you still would be a citizen.

Perhaps you came to America from another country. You and your family would like to live permanently in America. You receive a permit to live and work here. Time passes and you study the laws, duties, and rights of being a citizen of America. You take a test that covers information about America and your understanding of its laws and your duties. You pass. A judge will set a date and give you the oath of citizenship. You then become a citizen of America with all the rights, duties, and privileges of citizenship.

How Can My Values Affect My Citizenship?

You have seen in previous chapters how your values affect your behavior and attitudes toward self and others. Your values also affect how you act as a citizen. It is for you to decide to what extent your values will affect your citizenship. At times it will not be easy to act on your values. As you think about becoming involved as a citizen, think about what part your values will play.

Your Values Affect Your Attitudes Toward Government

You have learned that your values affect how you live with yourself and others. Your value of life influences its importance to you. The value you place on others influences your attitudes toward them. Your government is managed by a large number of citizens like you. The only difference is most of them are older and more mature. But they are no more a citizen than you are.

Things sometimes happen in government to cause you to doubt the honesty of some of its leaders. You may read in the papers about people in places of government leadership who are charged with some crime relating to a bribe, lying, immoral involvements, and fraud. This is serious. But you must remember that you have some of the same kinds of individuals in your town.

In deciding what you think and feel toward your government, look at the following statements. Place a check mark on the line under "Yes" or under "No" after each statement in the citizenship attitude questionnaire. These statements are about your values and how they affect your attitudes as a citizen. You are answering each statement based on how you see yourself now. Your answers may change as you grow older and become more involved.

Citizenship Attitude Questionnaire

Yes   *No*

____   ____   1.   As a citizen, I look for the best in my government leaders. (Value: Basic goodness of the individual.)

____ ____ 2. As a citizen, I do not judge a person's worth or effectiveness based on one incident of wrong doing. (Value: The dignity and worth of the individual.)

____ ____ 3. As a citizen, I do not judge my government based on the questionable actions of a few. (Value: Respect.)

____ ____ 4. As a citizen, I attempt to get all of the facts before arriving at a decision or judgment. (Value: Truth.)

____ ____ 5. As a citizen, I vote (or will vote when old enough) at every election—local, state, and national. (Value: Responsibility.)

____ ____ 6. As a citizen, I withhold judging a person until he/she has been proven guilty or innocent. (Value: Respect of individual rights and justice.)

____ ____ 7. As a citizen, I do not criticize others in public leadership roles until I have offered solutions and any help where I can. (Value: Personal involvement.)

____ ____ 8. As a citizen, I try to communicate my concerns to those who will listen and act. (Value: Recognition of those in leadership roles.)

Perhaps you have not given much attention to these areas of citizenship. This could be because you are just now reaching your teen years. If you are an older youth, you might have thought more about your attitudes toward your government. You look forward to voting for the first time and may wonder how your values may affect your decisions. You can already see that your values will affect your attitudes toward your government and its elected officials.

Your Values Affect Your Personal Concerns for Your Community

You may live in a town, a city, or in a rural area. Your values and your actions based on these values do affect your concerns for your community. Your community puts on a paper drive to help raise money to buy new play equipment for the park. Do you help? A local organization of your community needs teenagers to help with handicapped children on a trip to the zoo. Do you volunteer? Is it important to you to help with the children?

Your city officials, due to a water shortage, ask all residents to water their lawns only two days a week. Will you honor their request? A city ordinance was passed prohibiting hitchhiking on major streets of your city. Will you obey the new law? Your city decided that a youth committee was needed to help provide more citywide activities for youth. You are asked to serve. Will you accept?

Your Values Affect Your Personal Involvement As a Citizen

As you face these decisions or some just like them, you will become involved based on your values. Your concern for your community and ways you can be of help is determined by what you value—what is really important to you. You become involved when you are willing to act on your values.

Do you agree with the following statements?

1. A person ought to help others.
2. A person ought to try to love everybody.
3. The poor ought to be fed and clothed.

4. City government exists for the welfare of the residents.

5. Everyone can help make his community a better place to live.

You might have agreed with all five statements. But have you asked yourself, What have I personally done to make my community a better place to live? It is one thing to say you hold such and such a value; it is another to act on that value. Again you must decide. You must decide to:

—help with a paper drive.

—ride your bike in a bike-a-thon.

—hand out handbills for someone running for a local office.

—participate in "Clean-up Week."

—wash cars to raise money for a city youth center.

—vote your convictions when you are of voting age.

Your values and how you act on them will affect your citizenship. Your time and energy will play a part in deciding how much you can become involved.

What Should I Know About My Government?

You should know that your government is divided into local, state, and national governing units. You should know about your rights and duties as a citizen.

Your Local Government

The local government is city and county governments. Some city and county governments are combined to make just one government.

The mayor is usually the head of the local government. And usually a council of representatives work with the mayor. The local government is responsible for making decisions and passing laws or ordinances that affect the day-to-day operations of local government. You can find out about the local government by talking to someone at city hall or the county courthouse.

The police department, fire department, school board, and other organizations such as hospitals, libraries, and parks, are operated through the local government. Legal transactions about taxes and property are part of local government. If you talk with an official of your local government, you will find other ways that local government helps you.

Your State Government

Your state government is managed by a governor, a lieutenant governor, a senate, and a state house of representatives. The governor and his staff recommends new laws, expenditures, taxes, and policies to the representatives and senators for their approval. Many new state laws and policies are passed directly by the state representatives and senators. State government is big business. You are required to study about your own state government before you finish high school.

Your National Government

Your national government is run by the President, the House of Representatives, the Senate, and the Federal courts. These are referred to as the three branches of national government:

  executive—President and his staff;
  legislative—House of Representatives and Senate, referred to as the Congress of the United States; and
  judicial—All Federal courts with the Supreme Court of the United States being the last court of appeals.

These three branches and all their committees, boards, commissions, subdivisions, and departments are responsible for the management of the government of the United States of America. You also study about your national government in school. All of these branches of government are directed to follow the Constitution of the United States. This document gives guidance to the leaders of government.

The people of the United States elect the President, Vice-president, and all members of Congress. The President appoints those who are to serve as Federal judges. The appointments last for life. The United States Senate must approve all presidential appointments.

Your Rights and Duties

One thing you should know as a citizen is your rights and duties. The United States is a democracy—that means your country is governed by the people—based on the rule of law. The people elect the President and members of Congress to represent the best interests of all the people.

The Constitution, the highest law of the land, guarantees every citizen certain rights. These basic rights are found primarily in the Bill of Rights—the first ten amendments to the Constitution. Some of these rights are called civil rights. Read the Bill of Rights to find these rights.

You also have political rights. When you are eighteen years old, you will have the right to vote. You will be able to choose whom you would like to see in office and cast your vote for them. You will be able to vote in elections for school board members, state officials, and national leaders. You can vote for or against local taxes. You will have a political say on the issues that face your community, state, and nation. You also have the right to petition the government to do or not to do something. This is another way you can be heard by the leaders of your government.

The most important of your duties is to uphold the

Constitution and obey the laws passed by lawmakers. As you know, laws are passed by the elected officials to safeguard the lives, property, and rights of all citizens. Only by obeying the law can you be sure your rights will be protected.

Other duties include voting and a willingness to serve in the government. You may not be old enough for either of these now, but you will soon face these decisions. There are many vocations in which you might serve the government.

Do you think it is your duty to be loyal to your country? Would you accept the responsibility to defend your country in case of an enemy attack? Freedom and justice are important values of our nation. You cannot expect to exercise your rights if you are unwilling to accept your duties. Your values will help you make decisions regarding your involvement in your government.

What Part Should I Have in My Government?

You have already seen some things that you can do to have a part in your government. You may be twelve or you may be eighteen. The question is, What can you do now? You may ask another question, Is it really possible for young teenagers to become involved in their government process? Yes, it is. How? There are several ways that you can have a real part in your government.

Community Involvement

You can become a part of your local government by participating in the following ways.

1. Inform yourself on the local issues. You make a better volunteer when you know what and why you are doing a certain task.

2. Be willing to support local community-wide projects that affect the whole community. Time will not permit you to become involved in every project. Your values and concerns will help you decide which ones you want to help.

3. Study the candidates who are running for local office. Decide which ones you can support, and even though you are too young to vote, volunteer to help in their campaign. You could put up yard signs, make telephone calls, stuff and mail letters, type, enlist people to help, deliver circulars to homes, and many other such tasks.

4. Vote, if you are old enough. This is one of the best ways to be involved. Try to cast your vote intelligently.

5. Accept committee assignments at school and be willing to serve as an officer of local youth clubs or organizations.

These are but some of the ways you could become involved in the government of your community. You might know of other ways.

How can I get started? you may ask. You probably know some ways just by reading this chapter. Look at the list of ways below and add others to it.

1. Volunteer for committees and projects at your school, church, and community.

2. Call your mayor or one of the elected officials and volunteer your services for a specific project that has been announced.

3. Call your chosen candidate and volunteer to help his/her campaign.

4. Visit your city government offices and see how it is run on a day-to-day basis.

5. Study your community and see if there is an area of need; if so, do something about it. Bring it to the attention of community leaders.

Using your energy and time and applying your values in helping others can be very rewarding. You will find that it is hard work with little or no pay. It is up to you to decide just how big a part you want to have in your government.

What About Change in My Government?

A lot of things have happened through the years that cause questions to be asked about government and its leaders. Perhaps more than ever before in the history of the United States, its elected officials are coming under strict moral investigation.

This all adds up to needed change in government. Change raises more questions. Should you work for change? What part do Christian values play in changing the government? If you should work for change, how do you start? How do you decide if change is needed? All of these are important questions that you must decide to seek answers.

How Do I Decide If Change Is Needed?

Study the issues and policies present in local, state, and national governments. Compare your Christian values against those values you find in government. If you do not like what you find, then you have found out changes are needed. You may have found out that senior citizens living in nursing homes of your community are not receiving proper care. You may have found that changes in nursing home regulations are needed to correct the situation.

Another way to help you decide if change is needed is to look at those who are in office. What do they believe? What do they stand for? What values are they living by? How important are people to them? What is their voting record on key issues that are important to you? You may find that different persons could best represent you in several elected positions.

Deciding about change in government takes time and effort. You must first decide that it is important to you to know if change is needed. Then you must decide what responsibility you have in effecting change.

What Responsibility Do I Have for Change?

You are young. Perhaps you are still in your younger teen years. You wonder if you have any responsibility for change in your government. Even though you are not in a position of power or authority, you can find something to do.

You can be responsible for:

—speaking out to your friends and those in authority against policies that are not in harmony with your Christian values.

—helping those who live by Christian values to be elected to office. This way you can help make changes.

—reporting any immoral or illegal activities in your community so the authorities can correct the problems.

—your own behavior so that it agrees with your chosen values.

—serving in volunteer leadership positions in your community. This puts you in a position to help influence needed changes.

—writing letters to government officials to express your opinion.

As you grow older, your personal involvement will give you more opportunities to help make needed changes in your government.

Can Christian Values Influence Change?

Yes, they can. Your Christian values of love, respect, honesty, hard work, peace, faith, hope, kindness, and many others influence change in your government. The government will always need young Christian adults to serve in positions of leadership. In this way you will have an opportunity to live by your Christian values. It will not be easy.

There is a strong temptation by many people to set aside their Christian values when they attain places of leadership. You do not have to give up your values and convictions to serve your government. Those who stand for the right will be a great influence before others. At times you will be made fun of or laughed at. You will need to remember who you are. You will need to remember that as a Christian you represent Christ in everything you do and say.

Conclusion

Do not be timid in being a good citizen and a practicing Christian—they go together. Your citizenship was made possible by many human sacrifices. Your life as a Christian was made possible by the supreme sacrifice of Christ.

You alone must decide to what extent you will use your Christian life and Christian values to improve the quality of your government. Your values will conflict at times with new laws and new policies. You must then decide to take a stand for change or accept the situation as is. In cases of conflict, you may find that you sometimes have to weigh your rights against your duties to make a value judgment. You will find in the course of time that it is a real challenge to be a Christian citizen. Are you up to the task?

WHAT WOULD YOU DO?

"Citizenship"

It is Friday after school, and you are home alone. A friend calls you on the phone and asks, "What are you doing tomorrow?" You answer, "Nothing much. What's on your mind?" He says, "We need you to drive your pick-up truck tomorrow for the community paper drive. Will you help us?" He pauses for your answer.

What would you do?

Why?

What might be the results of your decision?

What else might you have done?

Do you think teenagers should accept some citizenship responsibilities? If so, why?

11

How Do I Value Myself?

"All my friends smoke and drink, so why shouldn't I?" (Girl, 14.)

"My mom and dad drink occasionally. They think it is OK for me to drink with my friends." (Boy, 16.)

"What harm is there in drinking? I know I can stop before I get drunk." (Boy, 16.)

"What business is it to anyone else if I use drugs? I am only hurting myself." (Girl, 15.)

"I know I am overweight, but no one likes me anyway." (Girl, 17.)

Do you value yourself as a person? In earlier chapters it has been pointed out that unless you have positive feelings about yourself, you will have difficulty thinking positively of others. You will have difficulty getting along with others.

Do you see yourself as a worthwhile individual? Do you see your ideas and opinions as being important? Are your beliefs, attitudes, and feelings just as important as your friends' values?

There are two ways to look at this. *First,* it is important that you question your ideas, thoughts, and opinions enough so that they make sense. They need to make sense when they are viewed in relation to all the facts in a given situation. *Second,* after getting all the facts, determining that your values make sense and are right for you, you must see them as worthy guides for your behavior.

This chapter will help you to think through how you value yourself as a person. It will also help you think about alcohol, other drugs, smoking, and poor eating habits. This chapter is to help you think about these things and their meaning to you personally.

In other sections of this book you have noticed that the decisions have been left up to you. You must decide for yourself. As you read this chapter, you will notice again that the decisions in the area of drinking, smoking, using drugs, overeating, or other habits like these are still up to you.

How Do My Values Affect the Habits I Form?

You have learned that values are those things that seem worthwhile to you. They are the ideas, thoughts, and feelings that guide your life. The things you value—such as home, family, church, honesty, friendship, trust, love, and many others—form guidelines that affect all of your life.

As you have grown, you have learned many things. You have learned some things so well that you do them almost without thinking. Habits are formed in this way. Anything you do repeatedly, almost automatically, is a habit. Some habits are positive; some are negative. That is, some habits are good for you; others are not so good. Going to bed at night is a positive habit. Nail biting is an example of a negative habit.

Habits are established because the performance of a particular behavior is pleasing in some way. You may not have been aware of why nail biting, for example, was pleasing; but for some reason it was. You learn to value anything that is pleasing or brings a sense of well-being. And because you value a particular behavior, you tend to repeat it. Therefore, a habit is formed.

Can you see how values lead to forming habits? Even things that are not enjoyed at first can become a repeated behavior, especially if you learn that they bring a sense of well-being. To break a habit formed in this way is very difficult.

You have probably formed many habits in your life. You will probably form many more. The following sections help you think about the habits you have formed and are forming with regard to your own personal appearance.

How Do My Values Affect My Personal Habits?

Take a look at yourself in a mirror. What do you see? You can answer that question by saying, "I really don't like what I see." "I'm overweight." "My face is a mess—with acne and all." "My hair looks lifeless and dull." Or you may answer that question by saying, "Well, I don't look so bad. I try to take care of myself with careful eating habits, habits of cleanliness, and exercise." Or you may say, "There are some improvements that need to be made. Maybe there are some things I can do to help."

Your appearance has changed a lot in the past few years. It will continue to change in the next few years. Along with a change in appearance, your attitudes toward yourself and your appearance have probably changed also. It has become more important to you to look good to others. You value a neat appearance. This causes you to spend more time bathing, washing your hair, and doing other things to improve your appearance. If you haven't given much thought to this, you may wish to start. Take a survey of yourself by noticing the following things: hair, complexion, teeth, fingernails, clothing, body odor, and posture.

The importance—value—you place on looking nice will determine the habits you form in taking care of yourself. For instance, bathing daily, shampooing your hair regularly, and brushing your teeth are examples of habits you can form that will make a positive improvement in your appearance.

Proper diet, exercise, and rest have something to do with your appearance also. What does your diet consist of? Do you eat mainly junk foods with little food value? Do you drink mostly soft drinks rather than fruit juices or beverages with food value and vitamins? If you are uncertain about what kinds of food will make a difference in your appearance, consult your family doctor. A nurse, a physical education teacher, a home economics teacher, or your mother might be able to guide you.

If you are overweight, underweight, or have severe skin problems, you need to consult a doctor for guidance. It is usually not a good idea to go on a diet without medical help. Fad diets or not eating can be harmful.

These things are related to the way you feel about yourself as a person. If you feel good about yourself and feel like a worthwhile individual, you probably have good health-care habits. When you feel pretty negative about yourself, you are likely not to care how you look. One girl said it this way: "If I don't like myself, then I don't think you will like me either. So if I am sloppy looking, I'll be sure you don't like me."

You can see how the way you value yourself as a person has something to do with the habits you form in taking care of yourself. Your body is God's gift to you. What you do with it is up to you. God's Spirit dwells with you if you are a believer. What kind of dwelling place does he have?

In the next section of this chapter you will read about tobacco, alcohol, and drugs. Beginning to use these can be habit-forming. As you consider the value you place upon yourself as a person, you need to consider what you will do about using chemicals that are potentially harmful to your body and to your personality.

What Shall I Do About Smoking, Alcohol, and Other Drugs?

At some time in your life, you will be called upon to make a decision concerning smoking, drinking alcoholic beverages, or using other drugs. Some people make a decision about these things early in life and stick with it throughout their lives. Other people make a decision each time an opportunity to use drugs, drink, or smoke comes along. In order to make any decision about these things, it is good to have as many facts as possible.

In the following sections, you will read about some of the effects of tobacco, alcohol, and other drugs upon your body. Perhaps this will aid you in deciding what to do.

Smoking

The facts about the hazards to your health of smoking are well known. There is enough concern about the possibility of smoking being harmful that a warning is printed on each package of cigarettes. Yet each year thousands of Americans begin smoking.

The teenage years seem to be a time when a person is likely to start smoking. You will have to decide whether you are proud enough of your body that you do not wish to take a chance on the health hazards of smoking. There are other considerations also. These will be discussed in the next section.

Drinking Alcoholic Beverages

Health hazards exist with drinking as well as smoking. Alcohol is a small molecule drug. As such it is capable of traveling throughout the body. There is no cell, tissue, or organ of the body that is unaffected by alcohol. The bones, the liver, the heart, the stomach, the intestines, the blood, the muscles, the kidneys, the nerves, and the brain are only a few of the parts of the body which will be affected, in time, by alcohol. It probably seems rather remote to you to consider the fact that by drinking a six-pack of beer per week you will eventually experience liver damage.

A much closer reality is that in any single drinking episode, if you consume an ounce of whiskey, one beer, or one glass of wine you will experience the effect of the alcohol on your brain. What happens? Moments after you take a sip of alcohol, a percentage of it goes directly into your bloodstream through the walls of your stomach. Moments later it enters the brain, where it does its work of depressing the action of the cells. In the brain are centers that control behavior. There are also centers that control reasoning and ability to make good judgments about behavior. These centers are the first areas of the brain to be affected by alcohol.

In other words, when you have had a beer or two, or a cocktail or a highball or two, you are no longer capable of making sound decisions. Alcohol has depressed these areas of the brain so that the alcohol is in control—not you.

At this point you usually have a sense of well-being. You may feel warm and friendly. You may be relaxed and more outgoing. Unfortunately, alcohol is a deceiver. You may mistakenly think that the alcohol is stimulating you. Alcohol is a depressant drug. If you continue to drink, your actions will become slower and slower, until you will eventually go to sleep. Or you may even pass out from the drinking.

The body gets rid of some of the alcohol that a person drinks through the lungs and kidneys. The rest must go through a process of oxidation (a chemical change in which the hydrogen is separated from the carbon and oxygen in the bloodstream). This process takes time. In the average-sized person, the body will burn up about one ounce of alcohol per hour. If you drink more than this in that length of time, there will be other physical effects, such as staggering, slurring of speech, or unsteady movements.

In young people, alcohol usually has a stronger effect than in adults. The reasons for this are not clear. However, body size and weight are contributing factors. The smaller the person, the greater the effect of the alcohol on his system. Another contributing factor is that young people expect to get a "buzz" or a decided effect from alcohol; therefore, they do.

Using Other Drugs

There are four major categories of drugs that are part of today's culture. They are as follows:

Hallucinogens—drugs which produce unreal fantasies, poor concentration, frequent changes in mood. Marijuana and LSD are drugs of this type.

Sedatives—these are drugs which slow down the activity of the central nervous system. Barbiturates and tranquilizers are two types of sedatives. These drugs depress both the body and the brain and have a calming effect on the emotions.

Stimulants—these drugs speed up the central nervous system. They seem to energize a person, make him wide-awake and full of pep.

Narcotics—these drugs are painkilling and sleep-producing drugs.

Sedatives, stimulants, narcotics, and alcohol are addictive drugs. That is, a person can get hooked on them so that his body is dependent. If he does not get the drugs, he goes through withdrawal. Withdrawal is a process that produces nausea, chills, fever, and physical pain. Withdrawal can even cause death.

It is not yet clearly known whether marijuana and other hallucinogens are addictive. Presently, it is thought that marijuana does not produce a physical dependence because a person does not experience withdrawal when he stops smoking marijuana.

The kind of effect that these drugs have on a person depends upon the kind of drug he uses. From the mild effects of marijuana to the hypnotic effects of the narcotic drugs (hard stuff), one may expect to experience slowing down, relaxation, a sense of calmness and well-being. The depressant drugs produce much the same effect as alcohol.

The stimulants cause a speeding up of the central nervous system. Heartbeat is more rapid, and blood pressure increases. The person may feel that he can take on tasks which are really beyond his strength. Usually stimulants produce a great amount of activity followed by exhaustion and a real "down" feeling.

These are only a few of the facts about the effects of smoking, drinking alcoholic beverages, and using drugs. If you are struggling with a decision about these, or if you have begun using any of these things, you will need to be sure you understand all the facts. You may want to ask yourself, "Am I happy with my decision?"

Besides the physical dependence tobacco, alcohol, and other drugs produce, there is also a psychological dependence. This means that the person *thinks* he must have the drug. He may think, for instance, that he must drink in order to be relaxed at a party or in order to be friendly. He may think that alcohol gives him self-confidence. He may think he has to have a tranquilizer to calm his nerves. This process of thinking about needing drugs or tobacco and the building up of a physical dependence is a combination that is hard to unlearn once it has become a part of a person's life.

There are many things to consider as you attempt to decide about smoking, drinking, or using drugs.

Why Do Teenagers Begin Smoking, Drinking, or Using Drugs?

"Hey, Tim, a bunch of us are getting together tomorrow night. We're going out to the lake, take a bunch of beer, and get smashed. How about coming along?"

"No, I don't think so, Greg."

"Why not? You'd like to have a good time, wouldn't you?"

"Yeah, sure, but I think I'll do something else."

"What would be more fun than getting smashed? We might even have a few joints. Come on, man, get with it. You're going to miss out on all the fun."

"Well . . ."

"You really don't have any reasons."

"I don't know."

"Sure you know. You know how much fun it will be. Might even be some girls there. All the guys who are *anybody* are going. Last time we asked you, you went. You sure are funny when you've had a couple of beers."

"Well, all right. I guess this time."

"Sure—you know you'll have a blast. No doubt about it."

"Yeah."

This conversation illustrates one reason why teenagers

start drinking. There is a lot of pressure from your peers to participate in the "fun." The same thing holds true for smoking and using other drugs. Your friends can put pressure on you to participate in activities that you really do not want to take part in. This is the reason some teenagers start smoking, or drinking, or using drugs.

Curiosity

Some individuals might begin smoking, drinking, or using drugs because they are curious. Being curious about the effects these will have on you, you may decide to try them. The effect of one cigarette or one drink usually varies with the individual. If a person is expecting a sensation of some kind, he will probably experience this sensation. If, for instance, he has heard that alcohol will give him a "buzz," he will probably experience that. This reinforces his curiosity. Now he no longer has heard about it, but has felt it for himself. His curiosity has been satisfied, and he may wish to repeat the experience.

This can happen even if the first experience a person has with a cigarette, an alcoholic beverage, or a drug is not good. He still wishes to find out if the good effects people tell him about are real. So he tries again. Still—just curious.

Social Custom

It seems that drinking and smoking are very much a part of the social custom in this country. Every sport event, every social event, and even many family events are always accompanied with plenty of liquor. Teenagers wish to be a part of the adult world, and the way to look sophisticated and grown-up is to participate in adult activities. Since these things are so much a part of the world you live in, it seems the "proper" thing to do.

Therefore, you may begin participating in smoking and drinking just to be a part of the social scene.

Defiance

If you have lived in a home or have been a part of a group where drinking and smoking are condemned as being "bad" and "bad for you," you may begin smoking or drinking to defy those in authority over you. You may think that a good way to get back at Mom and Dad for not allowing you to always have your way is to do something they do not approve of. Or you may wish to prove to others and to yourself that smoking and drinking are really not as bad as they may have said.

How Do I Decide?

In all areas discussed in this chapter—personal habits, personal appearance, habits of eating, exercising, rest, use of tobacco, alcohol, and other drugs—you must be the one to decide what you will do. Decisions about some of these things are difficult to make. Why? Pressure seems to come from every direction.

With the issue of drinking by itself, the pressures are many. Advertisements in magazines, in newspapers, and on television make it appear easy and attractive. Movies and television shows picture it as being the thing to do. Friends often put pressure on you to be part of the "fun" and "in" group by drinking. Family custom may indicate that drinking is OK.

To try to decide in the face of this kind of input can be a burden. Suppose, for instance, that you decide you will not drink. Can you withstand the social pressure that may come your way?

People who have made this decision have learned to value it and be able to say a firm no to the offer of a drink. Most of these people know the reasons why they refuse to drink. However, it is not necessary to give reasons. Just refusing by saying "No, thank you" in a firm and convincing manner is enough.

Suppose you decide to drink. What are some considerations that will be important? You may decide to drink only on special occasions and then to limit your intake in a manner that your body can handle. Drinking slowly and eating before and while drinking will help your body handle the alcohol. You may decide to drink only when you are relaxed and feeling well. This will avoid the possibility of drinking "to relax" and "to feel better."

You will also need to consider the effect of drinking and then driving. More than half of all fatalities in automobile accidents involve alcohol. A larger percentage than this of all automobile accidents involve alcohol. Be aware ahead of time of the potential dangers of drinking and then driving. You will need to make your decision about drinking and then driving ahead of time. Do not depend on your ability to make a rational decision while you are under the influence of alcohol.

Decisions about smoking will also come up from time to time. What will you do? Again, if you are sure of the facts and you have a good clear reason in your mind for not smoking, a firm "No, thank you" to the offer of a cigarette should be relatively easy. The same thing applies to using other drugs.

Some things to consider in deciding about smoking are as follows:

Do I smoke because it makes me feel grown-up and sophisticated? Is this a good reason to continue to smoke?

Do I smoke because I feel left out when all my friends are smoking? Why do I feel left out?

Is smoking really attractive? Is the smell of tobacco in my clothes, hair, and breath annoying to others?

Can I smoke only moderately, or will it become a habit I cannot control?

Deciding about using drugs is a serious matter. Not

only are most drugs addictive; many are illegal. To possess illegal drugs can get a person into serious trouble with the law. Furthermore, the kind of person you are determines whether you will use drugs. Your attitudes toward yourself and others have something to do with whether you use drugs and how they affect you if you do use them. If you have considered using drugs or are using them now, what are your reasons? Are you trying to escape or to belong? Are you trying to get turned on to life? Are you trying to defy your parents' or some other person's authority? Are these good reasons for putting yourself in a position to experience unpleasant and costly legal, mental, emotional, physical, and financial consequences?

To help you in your decision making, you may want to refer to chapter 3 and review the decision-making process of choosing, prizing, and acting.

WHAT WOULD YOU SAY?

"Pills and Booze"

It is Thursday, and you are just leaving your last class of the day. One of your friends that you have known for one semester walks up to you and says, "Say, a bunch of us are getting together tomorrow night for a party. You are invited—but bring your own booze. Another guy said he will have enough pills for everybody."

What do you tell him?

Why?

What other choices are open to you?

What might be the results of your decision?

Is it hard for you to say no? If so, why?

12

How Do I Value Things?

"Man, I wish I had a lot of money." (Teenage boy.)

"I never have any money." (Teenage girl.)

"I sure wish my dad made more money." (Teenage girl.)

"Money isn't everything in life." (Teenage boy.)

"I wish I had a lot of pretty clothes." (Teenage girl.)

"One of these days I am going to buy me a new car." (Teenage boy.)

"Make all you can, save all you can, and give all you can." (John Wesley.)

"Money never made a man happy yet, nor will it." (Benjamin Franklin.)

You can probably remember when you said some of the above statements yourself. Our society places a lot of emphasis on the value of money and things. Do any of the above statements reflect your own attitudes and feelings about the value and use of money? Just how important are money and things to you? You are faced with decisions about the use of money all the time. Your personal values will have a lot to do with your attitude toward money and things.

How Do I Value Money?

It is very important to you to have money to spend. But unless you are rich, you are limited in the amount you spend and save. You are under a lot of pressure from peers and society in general to spend your money in certain ways.

Your attitudes toward money. You get your attitudes toward money through experience of living and through your own values. You spend money in many different ways. Your family conditions also influence your attitude toward money. Your own parents' attitude toward money influences you. You may be from a family who has to be very careful about money. Or you may be from a family who gives you a generous allowance. You may be old enough to earn your own money to meet your personal needs. Maybe the following quiz will help you take a look at your present attitude toward money.

You and Your Money

To get an idea about your attitude toward money, complete this simple quiz. Write the number 5 on the line of the phrase that you would like to do most; write 4 on the line you would like to do next; 3 on the next; 2 on the next; and 1 on the line you would like to do least of all.

1. I would rather:
   ____ A.   Buy new clothes
   ____ B.   Go to a movie
   ____ C.   Give to my church
   ____ D.   Loan a friend money
   ____ E.   Put some money in my savings account.

2. I would rather:
   _____ A. Put a stereo on layaway
   _____ B. Go bowling
   _____ C. Give to my favorite charity
   _____ D. Buy a gift for a friend
   _____ E. Buy a United States savings bond.

3. I would rather:
   _____ A. Buy a new coat
   _____ B. Go skiing
   _____ C. Give money to World Hunger
   _____ D. Buy Mother a birthday gift
   _____ E. Invest some money in stocks.

4. I would rather:
   _____ A. Fix up my car
   _____ B. Go to a professional football game
   _____ C. Give money to the Red Cross
   _____ D. Buy something for a needy person
   _____ E. Save my money.

Now add up all the numbers that are on line "A" in each set. Add all the numbers on line "B" in each set, then lines "C," "D," and "E." Using the following chart, find out your attitudes toward money.

My Score	Attitude Emphasis
_____ "A" lines	Money is spent on *self* for *things* or *clothes*.
_____ "B" lines	Money is spent on *leisure* and *pleasure* for *self*.
_____ "C" lines	Money is *given* to different *religious* and other *helping* organizations.
_____ "D" lines	Money is spent on *others*.
_____ "E" lines	Money is saved.

Your highest score indicates your primary attitude toward your money at this time (it may change). Your next highest score indicates your secondary attitude toward your money. What did you find out? Were your scores close together? You may have found out that you were very close in two or more areas. Are you pleased with your present attitude or the emphasis you have toward money? Are you letting your values guide you? These are questions only you can answer.

Your Decisions Regarding Your Money

Do you decide to spend your money on something you *need* or something you *want?* At times you may find that your *wants* and *needs* are the same. Suppose you are out of blue jeans—you want a new pair and need a new pair.

Do you put the important things first in deciding how to spend your money? Do you save your money for such things as college, a car, or an expensive item you want? Perhaps you have so little money that these things are not being seriously considered at this time in your life. You think about having money to spend and decide what you would do if you had it. You are not alone in this—a lot of teenagers (and adults) do this all the time.

Your personal values will have a lot to do with your decisions regarding money. If you have a basic commitment to help others, you will use some of your money that way. If you think a Christian should give at least 10 percent to the church, then you will be guided by this value and give to your church. A deep respect and love for your friends will be another area where some of your money is spent. You will decide to buy them gifts. Having a generous spirit, loving your family and friends, possessing a willingness to help others, and supporting your church are all values that help you decide where some of your money goes. Your spending in these areas might not be much now. If you keep these same values and attitudes regarding your money when you grow older, you will find yourself doing much more in these same areas.

How Do I Value Things?

Your Possessions

What do you own? How did you get your possessions? Who paid for them? How important are they? Can you do without most of your possessions? What if a fire burned your house down? No one was hurt, but you lost all your things. How would you feel about that?

Just how would you rank your possessions? Why not find out by ranking from 1 to 10 the importance you place on the following? The number 1 is the most important item on the list, and the number 10 is the least important. Begin by placing the number 1 next to your first choice, 2 by your next choice, 3 by the next, and so forth, until you have ranked all ten items.

_____ 1. My clothes
_____ 2. My friends
_____ 3. My car or bike
_____ 4. My pet
_____ 5. My parents
_____ 6. My house
_____ 7. My church
_____ 8. My stamp collection
_____ 9. My stereo
_____ 10. My faith in God

How many "things" were high in your ranking? Where did you put your faith in God, family, friends, and church? If you placed them high on your list, is this where they really are in your everyday life and actions? What does it tell you if you ranked your clothes, a pet, your car, and your stereo as 1, 2, 3, and 4 in that order? Where would your emphasis or value be—on things?

Your Values and Things

You can begin to tell that the values you live by, those acted out each day, are the values that guide your decisions and emphases. Your values guide you in placing a low or high degree of importance on your possessions. If you have an ambition to make lots of money to buy things, then you value possessions to a high degree. If, on the other hand, you value your family, your friends, your church, and faith in God, then possessions or things are secondary to you.

At some time in your life you will come to understand what Jesus meant when he said, "Take heed, and beware of covetousness: for a man's life consisteth not in the abundance of the things which he possesseth" (Luke 12:15). Jesus was saying that you need to be careful not to place too much importance on the things you possess. When you do that the more important values of life are neglected—love, faith, hope, worship, and concern for others. How do your values affect the importance of things in your life?

How Do I Get My Money?

Allowance. As a young teenager it is hard to find a regular part-time job. Perhaps you are given an allowance by your parents. From this allowance you must provide most, if not all, your movie money, extra snacks at school, some clothes, and other personal items. You may be encouraged to save some of your money. Sometimes your allowance is based on your personal chores at home.

Part-time Job. Another source of money is your part-time job. This could consist of a paper route, baby-sitting, lawn mowing, or other odd jobs. If you are older (sixteen and above) you could get part-time work at fast food stores, other stores, service stations, and just about all kinds of odd jobs. When you work at a regular part-time job you will have more money to decide how to spend.

Gifts. Another source of money is gifts. Your gifts might be small, but they will amount to quite a lot during a course of a year. Family and friends give you money for special favors, birthday, Christmas, graduation, and just because they love you. Once in a while well-to-do grandparents will give you a rather large gift. They would like you to save it for college or other training for your future.

What Is My Buying Power?

You and your friends make up a large part of the "consumer market" (people who buy and use the products and services of others). As a result you and your friends have a large buying power. You are important to the makers of records, clothes, perfume, cosmetics, greeting cards, hair dryers, and books.

You and your peers own TV sets, record players, radios, cameras, and books by the millions. You play musical instruments and buy a large portion of the greeting cards and record albums. You purchase a large percent of the male sportswear and women's clothing. All this adds up to a lot of money—a lot of buying power. All this does not take into account the things purchased for you by family and other adults. You don't control their money or buying power.

What Influences My Buying?

You may feel you control your purchasing power. There are many pressures that cause you to buy the way you do. If you accept the fact that these pressures exist, you are on the way to becoming a more intelligent consumer. You will need to look for these pressures.

You are influenced by the manufacturer of products. Many manufacturers create new wants or new fads so they can sell you new products. Many of these new products do not last long. They are designed to last a short time or to become out of style. You are then forced into buying new products sooner. This is called planned obsolescence. It happens in the car industry—a new model every year. It happens in the fashion industry—new designs every year. It also happens to many of the products you buy. You are then influenced to buy the new product much sooner than you would like.

Television and radio also influence you to buy certain things. Many advertising commercials are aimed at you— the typical teenager. You should be aware of all the facts as you make decisions regarding the spending of your money. Do not be misled by incomplete reports of so-called facts. Check out the product before you buy it. Commercials will catch your attention but tell you little about the product.

You are influenced to buy things on an impulse. Store managers are aware of this and place colorful displays at checkout counters and cash registers. Just remember that all of the spur-of-the-moment purchases can quickly add up and wreck your budget.

Salespeople in the store where you shop influence your buying. They make you feel good by telling you that that coat looks great or that that dress is just right for you. Many of them get extra money or commission on all their sales. So be aware of the pressure salespersons place on you. Make sure you *need* or *want* the item and are not pressured into buying it.

Your friends also influence your buying power. Your friend Susan tells you of a neat new record album. You do not have it. Right away you want to go and buy one for yourself. Or you just heard about some brand-new posters your friends got at the shopping center. Off you go to get yours.

You can see that many people influence your buying, including your own family. You might find it a little hard to make a decision about spending your money when pressured by friends, salespeople, manufacturers, and all kinds of commercial advertisements. Again, your personal values ought to play a major part in how you spend your money.

How Can I Buy Wisely?

Another way your values can help you make decisions about your money is to help you buy wisely. If you have set some basic priorities in regard to your spending, you may want to work out a simple budget to guide you. Such a budget will keep you from overspending in one area and running short in another.

When you shop, be sure to compare items of the same size, quality, and price. Make sure you are getting a good item at a fair price. If it is guaranteed, be sure that you keep your proof of purchase. You will also need to check labels on everything you buy. Some items may be cheap but very expensive to clean or maintain.

Be sure that your values are more important to you than things. Know what you want and how to get it at a fair price. Practice comparison shopping when possible. If you do these things you are on your way to becoming a wise shopper.

What Relation Does Money Have to My Life Goals?

Do you value money as a means to accomplish certain life goals? Or do you value money for money's sake? You live in a materialistic society. That is, many people of your society place a great deal of importance on money and possessions. Your values and attitudes toward money and possessions will have a lot to do with establishing your life goals.

Some people take a strong stand against putting too much emphasis on earthly possessions. Your parents may have taught you this way. You may see in your own home that love, being at peace with each other, being happy, and serving Christ through his church are really where life's goals begin. For these goals to become yours, you must accept them and live by them.

Money is our way of exchange—money for goods and services. Your values will guide your attitudes, and they will affect the importance you place on money and possessions. This will be a growing experience for you. You will go through periods of trial and error. But if you know your life's true goals, then money and possessions will have their rightful place—and no more.

WHAT WOULD YOU DO?

"Five-Dollar Loan"

You just got paid from your part-time job. Bob, your friend, asked you for a five-dollar loan as you walked to your high school the next morning. Before you said anything, you remembered that Bob already owes you three dollars he borrowed last month.

What will you do?

Why?

What values do you use in arriving at your decision?

What other choices do you have?

What might be the results of your decision?

Is loaning your friends money a good policy? Why? Why not?

13

What About Values and Work?

"No thoroughly occupied man was ever yet very miserable." (L. E. London.)

"Since I was a little girl, I've always wanted to be a nurse." (Girl, 17.)

"I want a job that will make me happy. Money isn't all that important." (Boy, 17.)

"I want a job working outdoors. I couldn't stand staying inside all day every day." (Boy, 16.)

"Why should I be concerned about choosing a career? Wait until I get through college and then I'll decide what I want to do." (Boy, 16.)

"Me, work? I have the rest of my life to do that." (Boy, 15.)

"Yes, I have a part-time job. It gives me some extra spending money and a little experience." (Girl, 16.)

What are you going to be when you are grown? How many times have you been asked that question? Or what are you going to do when you get out of high school?

These questions or similar ones are about your life goals and ambitions concerning work.

Maybe you have been asked these questions and were not quite sure how to answer them. You have probably given some thought to the question "What are you going to be when you are grown?" Most boys and girls have. They even go through some rather interesting stages of development in making choices about their life's work.

How Do I Make Career Choices?

Choices about a vocation (life's work) are made over a period of years. As you experience your world, grow, and develop, you are learning things about yourself. You are also learning things about the people around you. You are learning what people do to make a living. You are learning whether or not they seem happy with their work. You are learning about the kinds of jobs or occupations that others seem to respect and admire.

You are also learning things about yourself that will influence your choice of a vocation. For instance, you are learning whether you would rather do things alone or with others. You learn whether you enjoy working with your hands or whether you would rather do the "thinking" and let others do the "making." Whether you enjoy being indoors or outdoors most of the time may come to influence your choice of work.

When you were younger you may have had some definite ideas about what you wanted to be when you grew up. Most little boys go through stages of wanting to be cowboys, policemen, firemen, or astronauts. Many little girls want to be nurses, teachers, or models. These choices are influenced by observation of parents and other adults in their world. Persons are influenced also by the things they read or see on television or in movies.

Now that you are a teenager, you are in another stage

of development as far as a choice of vocation is concerned. You will be exploring more fully the world of work. One way of doing this is through career classes at school. By your expanding contact with adults doing many kinds of jobs, you learn that there are many possibilities open to you. Some teenagers explore the world of work through actual work experience. Maybe you have had or will have several part-time jobs while going to high school. Or you may do volunteer work at a hospital, day-care center, or camp, or in some other way experience different kinds of work.

This exploring stage of vocational development will give you experiences that will help you narrow your choices. It will also help you know what you do and do not like to do. As you enter young adulthood, you will probably settle into some kind of work in your chosen field. Most people spend a number of years establishing and maintaining the career (field of work for which a person is especially trained or suited) they have chosen.

One of the determining factors about choosing your life's work is your attitude toward work itself. Do you mind working? Would it be hard for you to get up and go to work? Do you like to work at jobs that are dirty and messy? Does it bother you for your boss or manager to correct you when you are doing a lousy job?

Maybe you have not had an opportunity to learn all these things about yourself. However, finding out whether you can take orders without getting frustrated is important. Learning whether you can accept responsibility such as being on time, being willing to work a full day, and having pride in what you do are all important attitudes toward work. At some point in your life, you will face these questions about yourself and your attitudes toward work.

The purpose of this chapter is to assist you in examining

some factors that will help in making a career choice. You need information about yourself and about the possibilities for you that will, at least, help you get started.

A choice of career is one of the most important decisions in a person's life. It is a complicated choice for many people. You may need some help in choosing. What you read here will help. Afterward you may want to talk with a counselor at school or with someone on your church staff who can further help you.

What Are My Life Goals?

Any discussion of career choice must include a discussion of goals. What are your goals? What do you have in mind for yourself in the future? You will work hard to reach any goal that you believe in strongly. In order to establish some meaningful goals, you will want to look at your *needs* and your *values.*

First, your *needs* are those things you must have to keep you alive and going as a person. You must have food and water, for example. These are examples of physical needs you have. You also have other needs. You need to feel safe and secure. You need to feel loved, and you need to feel that you are a worthwhile person in your own eyes and in the eyes of others.

These needs are motivators. They cause you to behave in ways that will meet these needs. They help you set goals for reaching them. So your needs help determine the goals you set for yourself.

Your *values* also help determine the goals you set. Values are those things that seem important and worthwhile to you. You may value being with people. In turn, being with people may satisfy your need to feel good about yourself and to have others feel good about you. In setting a goal for your life you may want to be sure that your goal includes being with other people.

How would this affect career choice? A person who values being with others and needs other people in his life might not be happy as an automobile painter, where most of his energy is spent in working with "things." A decision to be a flight attendant, on the other hand, might satisfy the need to be with other people and to have others feel good about you. This is only one example of how needs and values help you to set your life goals.

Kinds of Goals

There are two different kinds of goals: long-range goals and short-range goals. You will need to know the difference between these kinds of goals and how to go about deciding what your goals are.

Long-range goals. As a teenager, you are probably beginning to think more about the future than you did when you were younger.

You are thinking about such things as: Will I get married? Whom will I marry? Do I want to be a father or mother? Do I want to earn a lot of money? Do I want to live in the biggest house on the street and drive the best car? Do I want to go live by myself in an apartment in a big city? Do I want to go live in the mountains and ski and backpack the rest of my life?

These kinds of questions are asked by people who are searching for long-range goals. The goals you set help determine the kind of life you will eventually have. An exciting life, family security, comfort, happiness, and social recognition are all examples of long-range goals you may have.

Short-range goals. These goals are the characteristics you will need in order to reach a long-range goal. Think back to a time when you reached a goal you had been working on. What helped you reach these goals? Skill? Understanding the job? Freedom to do it your way? Determination? Being helpful to someone else? Honesty? Feeling secure in doing it? Gaining respect of others? Learning something new? These are all examples of the kinds of things you will need to feel or develop in order to reach your long-range goals.

If you want to be the president of a big company, for instance, that is a long-range goal. In addition, you will probably decide that you also want social recognition and to earn a lot of money. In order to reach these goals, some other goals—short-range goals—must be set early in life and reached. You will probably need to be honest, be responsible, have determination, and enjoy being independent in your work. A person with goals like these, who starts early enough in life, can probably reach his long-range goals.

Goals give your life a sense of direction and purpose. Think about the goals you have set for yourself today. What are your goals for the week? What about the future? If you have set some goals for yourself, the next step is attempting to reach them.

How Do I Decide Where to Work?

Besides thinking about your life goals, there are other things you need to consider in making a decision about your life's work. In this section, you will look at characteristics you have which help you to decide about your life's work. You will also look at characteristics of the vocation and how these affect your decisions.

Your Characteristics

Interests. One thing that is important in helping you decide what vocation you want to follow is interest. You have many interests. If you were asked to name some things you are interested in you might name some sport, an activity you particularly like, or a subject in school.

You might even name a person you are interested in.

Maybe you have difficulty naming things you are interested in. If you do, you might find clues to your interests by considering what you do in your spare time. Interests are expressed in other ways also. You may be interested in reading about a particular subject or in watching a particular event but not participating in it. Interests can be expressed by what a person does or by a feeling he has about a certain thing.

Interests are important in considering a job choice. Since you, like most people, will probably spend at least eight hours per day, thirty to forty hours per week for the next forty or fifty years, in some kind of job, you will want to be interested in what you are doing. Some people are interested in their jobs only because it provides a steady paycheck. This paycheck, in turn, buys the things they need and value. Some people are interested in their job because it brings much personal satisfaction. These people might work at their job even if they were not paid. Your interests will affect your choice of a job and will affect your satisfaction with the job.

Abilities. Those things that you can do well are your abilities. You have many abilities. You may be good at math; if so, you could say you have good math ability. You may be good at doing things with your hands, or you may be good in art or music. If this is true, you could say you have ability in these things.

Ability is important in the choice of a vocation. A person who has little numerical ability (ability to work easily with numbers) would be unsuited for a job as a mathematician. On the other hand, a person who has good ability to express himself in words—that is, he can write well, read well, and talk well—would do well in a job requiring these abilities. A journalist or an English teacher are examples of these kinds of jobs.

You have many abilities and so are suited for a number of different jobs. Many abilities that you have you may not be aware of because you have not had a chance to develop them. Besides your known abilities, you may have the capacities to learn certain other things. These capacities or potentialities are called aptitudes.

Aptitudes. Those things for which you have a capacity to learn or a potential for doing are called your aptitudes. Generally, people can learn easily something for which they have an aptitude. Going back to the example of a person with good numerical ability, it could be stated that the person had a good aptitude for mathematics.

You may have aptitudes for many kinds of things. You may have aptitudes for the kinds of things that you learn in school. Some people have an aptitude for understanding machines and working with them. The various aptitudes you have are important in the kinds of work you may choose to do.

If you would like to know more about yourself—your interests, your abilities, your aptitudes—and how these can lead to satisfying decisions about your choice of career, your school counselor can help.

Job Characteristics

As was mentioned earlier, in order to make good decisions about a vocation, you need to consider some characteristics of the vocation. In this section there will be a discussion of some general considerations concerning jobs.

Availability. Teenagers who are thinking about careers and vocations like to read about and learn about many different kinds of careers. Not all the careers that you read about and learn about are readily available. A career as an astronaut, for example, is very limited. Only a select few ever get to be astronauts, while many thousands may wish to be.

Other vocations have limited availability. Some may be limited to select people. Others may be limited to certain locations. An oceanographer, for example, would be employed only in specific parts of the country, as would a forest ranger. A person desiring to enter these vocations might have to move far away from family and friends.

You may wish to enter a vocation which may take years to achieve. Medical doctors and particularly those who specialize in one area of treatment are examples. Then after years of training, you may have to move to a faraway city where your specialty can be practiced.

The availability of jobs is affected also by the number of people entering that vocation. Certain fields tend to always have more than enough qualified people to fill the jobs that are open and available. Teaching and engineering are examples of these fields. Other fields seem to have more openings for people to get a job than there are qualified people to fill these jobs.

When considering a certain vocation, you will need to check into the availability of jobs in that field. Questions you will want to ask include such things as:

Are there actually jobs available in this field?

Are the jobs that are available located in the section of the country where I live?

Do I want to move to the part of the country where the jobs are available?

If the job calls for many years of training, will there still be job openings when I have completed the training?

What about jobs of the future? What are the areas of greatest potential for me?

Respectability.   What is a respectable job? This is answered differently by different people. It takes many thousands of kinds of jobs and workers to run the thousands of industries in this country. It takes all kinds of jobs and workers to keep this country going and to keep the citizens living the kinds of lives they do. Any kind of job which is useful in helping to maintain a standard of living for himself or others is a respectable job.

Respectability means different things to different people. Probably the key to deciding whether a job is respectable is to ask a person performing that job how he feels about himself as a person while performing the job. If he feels good about himself, then his job is respectable. The only exceptions to this would be those jobs which are actually harmful to others even though the person performing it may feel good about himself while doing it.

Occupational values. Many other job characteristics may be important to you as you choose your life's work. Below is a list of things that might be important. From this list consider the factors that seem most important to you. If you have a job that fits your values, you will be more likely to succeed and be happy in your job.

Characteristics of a job which I would value the most are:

1. Feeling of accomplishing something
2. A challenge to use my abilities
3. Freedom to be creative (making new things or doing things a new way)
4. Work that involves excitement
5. Work that provides new situations daily
6. Working with things
7. Working with other people
8. Working with ideas
9. Outdoor work
10. Work where I am a member of a group or team

11. Work where I am alone or independent of others
12. Good working hours
13. Control over others
14. Good pay
15. Work where I have a chance to advance and get a better job
16. A job where I can work at my own pace
17. Work that is more or less the same each day
18. Work in the city of my choice
19. Work that provides prestige (high esteem) in the community
20. Work where I am able to express myself.

You can see from this list of occupational values that there are many things to consider in planning for a career. The more you understand and know about the job characteristics involved and how important these are to you, the more wisely you can plan. Occupational information is available that will help you discover the characteristics of the jobs you are interested in. Your school counselor can help you locate this information.

Why Are My Career Decisions Important?

You may be thinking by now that there are too many things to keep in mind in making a career choice. You may be saying, "Why can't I just look in the paper, find an ad about a job, apply for it, and go to work?" You may be able to do that, but there is a lot of competition for most jobs. The person who is best qualified for the job is usually hired. Even if you were hired, how do you know you would feel satisfied enough with the job to stay with it?

Career decisions are not easy to make. There are many thousands of jobs to choose from. There are many jobs that each individual is capable of doing. There are many jobs that you would enjoy doing. There are many new kinds of jobs being created all the time. Jobs that were once thought of as men's work are now sometimes done by women. The same is true for jobs that were once done only by women. All these facts make career decisions difficult but important.

Career decisions may be thought of as a process (continuing) rather than a once-and-for-all decision. They are usually made a step at a time rather than all at once. You began making decisions leading you toward your life's work when you were a small child.

The subjects you take in school are a step along the way. The way you explore and expand your knowledge of vocations is another step along the way. You will have many decisions to make that are related to your life's work. Whether or not to go to college, to get additional training for a job outside of college, to go to work immediately after high school or while still in high school are examples.

You may wish to pursue one career for a few years and then change to another. In a country like the United States you are free to do that, and it is entirely possible to do so. Decisions such as these can be made by using the same steps that were described in chapter 3.

One final word. If you have not made a career choice by the time you are through high school, you are not alone. Many teenagers have not. The exploratory period sometimes lasts through college. Also, don't think that your choice of career must be your last choice. Later in life, you may have a chance to make some other decisions about your career. Learn all you can about yourself and about the world around you. This will give you a better chance of making wise choices leading to a satisfying life.

OPEN-ENDED STATEMENTS

"My Goals and Skills"

Complete the following statements about yourself in regard to your goals and skills.

1. I will finish _____
_____.

2. I have a goal to _____
_____.

3. I can make _____
_____.

4. I can build _____
_____.

5. I want to become _____
_____.

6. I can fix _____
_____.

7. I am good at _____
_____.

8. I know a lot about _____
_____.

14

Where Do I Go From Here?

"For the first time my life seems to have some direction to it." (Teenage boy.)

"I guess I am growing up—I am beginning to understand my parents better." (Teenage girl.)

"At times I feel I am going nowhere with my life." (Teenage boy.)

"Some decisions I face are hard. I just don't know what to do." (Teenage girl.)

"Our yesterdays follow us; they constitute our life, and they give character and force and meaning to our present deeds." (Joseph Parker.)

"But seek ye first the kingdom of God, and his righteousness; and all these things shall be added unto you." (Matt. 6:33.)

Most of your life stretches out before you. As represented by the statements above, you may feel a sense of direction for your life. Or you may feel a real sense of frustration about your life. You sometimes wonder about your values, your life goals, and your faith in God.

Perhaps you feel that growing into young adulthood is not that easy after all. You have many questions that go unanswered. Inside of you there are desires, feelings, and drives you want to express and satisfy.

Sometimes you think to yourself, *Why do I have to wait for some of life's experiences? Why can't I have them now?* Would you want life to take a big jump in time so you could have all the experiences and responsibilities that go with adulthood? At other times you may think to yourself, *I am happy being a teenager. I have my family, my friends, and my church. I will take life as it comes to me.*

The purpose of this chapter is to put into summary fashion some of the questions that have been discussed in this book. What is important to me? What kind of life-style do I want? Do I need to make some personal changes in my life? Where do I go for help? How do I get the most out of life? What decisions do I face now?

What Is Important to Me?

As you examine your life's values, you may conclude that many things are important to you. You may decide that life itself is the most important thing you have. Or you may think that your faith in God is above all else. Other things are also important, such as your family, your friends, your personal values, and your possessions. In trying to decide what is really important to you, take these two steps: Clarify your values and set personal goals.

Clarify Your Personal Values

Before you go any further in life, be willing to stop and ask yourself, *Really, now, what are my true values?* To clarify your values is to focus on them in the light of your behavior. It will be difficult for you to know what

is important to you if you don't know what you value.
Ask yourself, *Are my values coming through to others?*
or *Can my family and friends tell what is important
to me by my everyday actions?*

Your values are building blocks for your personal effectiveness as a human being. They act as guides to abundant
living. They also act as warning signs against immorality.
You start with a basic set of life values and build your
life on these values. Some of these values are absolutes;
that is, they are part of God's revelation and law to us.
Others are society's which you will test by experience
and by the Bible.

You need to feel important to yourself. You are indeed
someone very important. You have many opportunities
to test and clarify your values every day you live. Through
these experiences you will find yourself discarding negative values and building on those that are positive. Knowing your values and living by them will help you find
out what really is important to you.

Set Personal Goals

Your goals need not be complicated. Set goals that you
are able to do. Set your goals in the right time period.
Give yourself plenty of time to accomplish the larger
goals of life. Set just a few personal goals at one time.
A lot of frustration comes when you set too many goals.
It's too big for you. You tend to give up.

Set your goals that are basic to your life and skills. Set
goals regarding your work experiences; your education,
high school and further training; your personal growth;
your hobbies or interests; your friendships; and your spiritual growth.

These are the areas where life finds you at this time.
Keep just a few goals in front of you and do your best
with them. When you finish one, then set another that

is important to you. Remember these guidelines when you are trying to set your goals:

1. Understand your goal.
2. Believe in your goal.
3. Make sure your goal is realistic.
4. Make your goal a clear-cut choice.
5. Be sure your goal can be achieved in a measurable length of time.
   A. Short-term goal—month or less
   B. Intermediate goal—a month but less than a year
   C. Long-range goal—over a year
6. Ask yourself, *Do I really want to do this?* If the answer is yes, go at it. If not, then forget it.

Clarifying your values and setting personal goals will assist you in finding out what really is important to you. And once you solve this problem, you will begin to discover where you are headed in life.

What Kind of Life-style Do I Want?

What life-styles are open to me? You can choose a life-style that has its emphasis on getting material things. You could choose a life-style that places emphasis on pleasure. You could choose a life-style of crime and immorality. You could choose a life-style of just being a bum—no roots anywhere. You could choose a life-style that is very religious in nature. You could choose a life-style that is properly balanced between the worship of God, work, pleasure, service to others, and family. Whatever life-style you choose should be in harmony with your values.

Which life-style do I choose? Only you can make that decision. You may choose one life-style and later discard it. Why? Because you may find out it is in conflict with your values and beliefs. Choosing a life-style should be done on the basis of what you are going to do with your life. What do you want to accomplish? Do you want to be a nurse, a minister, a salesman, or a bookkeeper? Your life's vocation will play a part in your choice of a basic life-style. Choosing the right life-style for you will give direction to your life.

Do I Need to Make Some Changes?

Do I need to change some personal values? Do you have some values that are causing you trouble or problems? Are you taking good care of your body? If not, maybe you need to make a change. Are you placing a lot of importance on drink and drugs? If so, maybe you need to consider some value changes. Are you having problems of being selfish toward others? Maybe a change is in order. You must take a long look at your personal values and see if you need to make some changes. You must want to make them yourself. You make them because it is important to you to do so.

Do I need to change some attitudes? Your values reflect your attitudes. Look at the way you respond to people. Are you pleased with what you see? If not, maybe a change is in order. Think how you talk about certain people. Do you feel proud of this? If not, maybe you need to consider changing your attitude in this area. What about your attitude toward your parents and family? Is a change needed here? How do you treat your friends? Do you think they are pleased with your attitudes? These questions are for you to answer. It may be that you need a change in only one area. Are you willing to make that change? You decide.

Do I need to change my behavior? Are you mad a lot? Do you break or kick things? Do you get upset easily and lash out at people? Do you talk back to your parents? Does it really matter if you do your homework? As a

Christian, do you take God's name in vain? Do you get upset when asked to clean your room, making a big hassle out of it? Occasionally you might want to stop and evaluate your behavior in light of what you say are your values. If you find that your behavior conflicts with your values, you might consider some changes.

Do I need to change my friendships? Choosing the right group of friends is important to your spiritual, emotional, intellectual, and moral growth. How do you see your friends? Do they hold to the same values as you? Do your friends pressure you into doing things that are against your values and beliefs? Can you say no when saying so is right for you? Will your friends accept your no without putting too much pressure on you to change your mind? Is it harder for you to tell some friends no than others? Maybe these questions cause you to take a survey of your friendships.

You may find that you need to break some friendships and make some new ones. You may find after a close evaluation that some of your friends do not stand for the same things that you do. You also may find that you are permitting some of your friends to exert too much pressure on your personal decisions.

Getting self together for life and living may include some important changes in your life. Being willing to make these changes is where you are right now. You cannot expect others to change your personal values. You don't want others changing your attitudes and behavior. You are the only one who can make changes in your friendships. Life is full of decisions that are yours alone. Decide in the best interests of your own life and others.

Where Do I Go for Help?

All people need various kinds of help throughout the course of life. You are no exception. Living out your day-to-day life is too big a task alone. You need help from time to time with all sorts of problems and questions. You may say, "That's right, but where do I get it?" You desire help with your personal problems and needs. You are faced with spiritual needs that deserve answers. You wonder about what you are going to do and be in life. All of these areas are important to you, and you want help from time to time. There are some individuals in your life who are ready to listen and to help you.

Your parents. Yes, that's right. Your parents are the best friends you have. Be sure to keep open the communication line with your parents. Share your problems and needs with them. Let them know what is bothering you. Talk with them about everything that is important to you. Confide in them the desires and ambitions of your life. Don't be afraid to ask them questions about life and living. Remember, they want to help you. Your parents want you to have a happy and rewarding life.

Other members of your family. You may have a hard time sharing your needs and problems with your parents. If so, perhaps you have an understanding older sister or brother that you could share with. You may have grand-parents whom you have come to love and appreciate very deeply. Share with them your needs, problems, and questions. You may find that they have a great deal to offer or some good suggestions for you to think about. You may turn to an aunt or uncle.

Your pastor. Another source of help for you is your pastor or a friend who is a minister. They stand ready to help you and to listen to your needs and hurts. They will also recommend other counselors who work with youth in all problem areas. Your pastor or minister is a good source of help for you. Most of them will truly try to understand *you* and *your* areas of need.

Your teacher. Not just any teacher, but the one who

is very special to you. This person could be your Sunday School teacher, your math teacher, or your social studies teacher. Whoever it is, she or he will have your best interests at heart. There will be a real trust and confidence level built up between the two of you. You feel somewhat at ease in sharing with this special person.

A special friend. For a growing teenager, a special friend is the best source of help to share needs and problems. You can sit down with your special friend and just talk things over. This experience helps you to get things out in the open. It will help you to get a different look at your feelings and concerns. This doesn't mean to say that your special friend has all the answers. You may need to seek adult counseling and guidance.

You live in this world. You are not alone. Others are all around you. As you live out your life, you will find that from time to time you will reach out to some caring person who will help you in time of need. The secret to this is that you must do the reaching out for the help. You must decide you want help and guidance for your life. Life is too short and precious for you to need help and not ask for it. Talk to people who care about you. Share with them your personal, spiritual, and vocational problems. Ask your questions; they might not have all the answers, but they do care about your welfare.

How Do I Get the Most Out of Life?

Teenagers like you have been asking that question for a long time. Adults ask it too. There is no comprehensive set of answers. The answer to this question depends largely on what you are willing to put into life. Even though it is hard to answer this question, there seem to be a few basic guidelines that you may consider.

Have faith in God. Do not be ashamed to accept Christ as your personal Savior. In doing so, you make peace with God and become a member of God's larger family of Christians. Let your faith grow through Bible study, worship, and praise to God. Let your everyday life be a testimony that you belong to God. This is where life and living really start.

Be at peace with yourself. Make sure your behavior is consistent with your values. Be happy about yourself. Love yourself because you see things in you that are right and good. Make sure that what goes into your mind and body is best for you. Be proud of what you stand for and what you are. Being at peace with yourself is feeling a sense of direction for your life.

Be at peace with others. It will be difficult for you to get the most out of life when you are not at peace with others. Try not to hold grudges. Seek to settle any interpersonal problems quickly. Be more than willing to act first in making things right with family and friends. One sure way to be at peace with others is to be a peaceable person yourself. Desire that kind of character trait for your own personality. Our society needs peacemakers.

Maintain a positive outlook on life. Look on the bright side of things. Don't be caught up in playing the "poor me" game. If things aren't as you want them to be—change the situation! Do something about it. Make things happen through hard work, right planning, and positive thinking. Don't give up on anything until you have given it your best try.

Become dedicated to a worthwhile cause. Seek a cause bigger than self. You may feel that God wants you to become a minister, a missionary, or a medical doctor. Your worthwhile cause may be different from your regular vocation. You may become a truck driver but be dedicated to helping needy boys find a better way of life. You may become a nurse but be dedicated to helping starving children of the world. The cause you seek should be a real need. It should be done with no thought of any personal return except the inner peace of feeling you helped somebody else. Whatever causes you find, put your heart into it. Be sincere about your motives. Your own works will follow you.

These guidelines are briefly stated. You can enlarge the concepts to include all your life and endeavors. Be willing to put more into life than you hope to get out of it, and you will find that you get out more than you feel you put in.

Conclusion

Most of your life is out before you. You are young now. You have a lot of living to do. You are faced with many everyday kinds of decisions. You are also faced with more serious decisions about your spiritual growth. You are faced with vocational decisions. In time you will be faced with the decision of choosing a mate.

As you face all of these decisions, let your values and beliefs play an important role. Decide now that you want to become what God intended you to be—a Christian first and a productive citizen second. Begin now by making the right choices for you. Clarify your values. Examine your attitudes and behavior. Make the changes you feel you need to make. Learn from your mistakes. Remember, if you work at the job, you can "get yourself together" for a full and meaningful life. May it be so for *you!*

OPEN-ENDED SENTENCES

"When I Am Eighteen"

Complete the following open-ended sentences, telling in each something you are going to do when you become eighteen or over.

1. When I am eighteen, I am going _____
   _____.

2. When I am eighteen, I will _____
   _____.

3. When I am eighteen, I plan to _____
   _____.

4. When I am eighteen, I know I _____
   _____.

5. When I am eighteen, I am going _____
   _____.